# Writing Workshop

# Writing Workshop

## THE ESSENTIAL GUIDE

*Ralph Fletcher*
*JoAnn Portalupi*

**HEINEMANN**
Portsmouth, NH

**Heinemann**

361 Hanover Street
Portsmouth, NH 03801-3912
www.heinemann.com

*Offices and agents throughout the world*

**Library of Congress Cataloging-in-Publication Data**

Fletcher, Ralph J.
    Writing workshop : the essential guide / Ralph Fletcher and JoAnn Portalupi.
      p. cm.
    Includes bibliographical references.
    ISBN 0-325-00362-9 (alk. paper)
      1. English language—Composition and exercises—Study and teaching.
    2. Forums (Discussion and debate).   3. Authorship—Collaboration.
    4. Group work in education.   I. Portalupi, JoAnn.   II. Title.

LB1576 .F48422 2001
372.62'3044—dc21                               2001039161

*Editor:* Lois Bridges
*Production editor:* Sonja S. Chapman
*Cover design:* Ellen Korey-Lie
*Interior design:* Cathy Hawkes, Cat & Mouse Design
*Manufacturing:* Louise Richardson

Printed in the United States of America on acid-free paper
    09  RRD                19  20

For the new generation of teachers:

You will have a greater impact
on the life of this nation
than you can imagine.

# Contents

## Appendixes

# Acknowledgments

There are countless friends, teachers, and children who, directly or indirectly, shaped this book. We'd like to give special thanks to Lois Bridges, who persistently and patiently prodded us throughout this project. We wrote a much better book than we could ever have written without her. She did that magical thing in which an editor steps into the writers' vision and sees more in the project than they can see themselves. This is a wonderfully intimate kind of dance, and we feel lucky to have had her as a partner.

# Introduction

We were talking with Jeremy, a second grader and friend of the family, who had just returned from visiting Disney World. There he sat at our table, excitedly talking, barely stopping to breathe. He spilled out a wealth of inside information—which rides to go on (or avoid), how to use the new Fast Pass system for the most popular rides, food, etc.

"You should write about it," I (Ralph) urged.

He gave me a questioning look.

"You could write a guidebook," I suggested. "It would give tips so other kids would know what to do when they go to Disney World."

"But who would read it?" Jeremy asked. He quickly dismissed the idea and continued talking about his vacation.

At this point we (the two authors of this book) exchanged a significant look. We know that Jeremy participates in a second-grade class in which kids do write frequently. But nearly all the writing is assigned by the teacher. There is no writing workshop and, consequently, Jeremy doesn't really see himself as a writer. He certainly doesn't have a strong sense of audience, real readers who might be interested in the words, ideas, and information he puts on paper.

It is customary to select an inspirational story or anecdote to begin a book such as this one. But this story about Jeremy is important because it clearly illuminates several things we believe in our deepest bones. Kids in writing workshops *do* see themselves as writers. They develop a genuine feel for writing—its power and purpose. They know what it means to write for themselves—in a writer's notebook, for example—but they also know what it means to write for an audience of interested readers. They understand the heavy lifting that writing does in the real world.

This doesn't happen by magic. It happens because teachers create a unique environment where students get to walk in the shoes of writers nearly every day.

Since 1980 we have been helping teachers implement the writing workshop. Is writing workshop the only way to teach writing? Of course not. A sampling from different school districts will show a variety of approaches and programs. But none of them matches the writing workshop when it comes to growing strong writers.

# How to Read This Book

Instead of trying to write an encyclopedic, everything-you-ever-wanted-to-know book about writing workshop, we have worked hard to boil the subject down to the essentials. We wove in theory when it seemed appropriate to explain the roots of a particular idea. But we kept our focus on writing a practical book that would clearly show how any teacher could implement this approach.

In the first short chapter, we bring in several different examples to give you the feel of a writing workshop. After that we slow the book down and provide chapters that give an in-depth look at particular aspects of the workshop—time and space, writing conferences, the writing cycle, and so forth.

It is instructive to take apart a watch and closely examine all those shiny gears and springs. But there is always the danger that you'll never be able to get all the pieces back together again. Our goal is to leave you with a sense of the writing workshop in its entirety, ticking, humming.

The writing workshop is not foolproof. Unless you are very lucky, chances are you will run into particular bugs or glitches as you get started. We troubleshoot these potential potholes in Chapter 10. The Appendixes consist of a number of practical forms and other resources that we have found useful in making the workshop run smoothly.

At the supermarket you can purchase a taco "dinner in a box," which includes a dozen tacos shells, seasoning for the meat, and spicy sauce to go on top. The advertising, of course, is a bit misleading: the meat, cheese, and lettuce are essential ingredients for a complete meal, but these items must be purchased separately.

Is this book "workshop in a box"? Yes and no. We have tried to provide the most important tools you'll need to get your workshop up and running. But there are a few ingredients we cannot provide, and the most important one of these is you, the teacher. Your passion, patience, humor, your faith in the writers you work with, will be crucial to making your writing workshop come alive.

Writing is tremendously important. Every one of our students will need to travel down the long road of written communication as we enter the twenty-first century. Our twenty-plus years of working with teachers has convinced us that the writing workshop gives our students the very best tools to move confidently down that road. This book is the culmination of our efforts, a synthesis of our best thinking on this idea. We invite you to travel down the road with us as we explore together a potent tool for empowering young writers.

# The Writing Workshop

W hat is writing? We might define it as the skill of writing down particular words, in a particular order, to create particular effects. Students will use writing in countless ways: to communicate, express, question, persuade, synthesize, teach. It takes years to gain control and mastery over written language. But students who learn to write well truly have one of the most powerful tools imaginable. And it is something that nobody can take away from them.

Teaching kids how to write is hard. That's because writing is not so much one skill as a *bundle* of skills that includes sequencing, spelling, rereading, and supporting big ideas with examples. But these skills are teachable. And we believe that a writing workshop creates an environment where students can acquire these skills, along with the fluency, confidence, and desire to see themselves as writers.

What does a writing workshop feel like? Imagine a junior high industrial arts class. Kids wearing goggles are spread out around the room, each working on their individual projects. The instructor gathers the students for a few minutes to point out technique, or remind them about a safety issue. But pretty soon the kids are back working on their own projects. The room is noisy and dirty. With each kid working at a different pace, on a different part of his or her project, the atmosphere seems disorganized at first glance. But on closer study, you can see that a lot is getting done. While the students work, the instructor moves around the room, examining, complimenting, asking questions, making suggestions. At times the instructor picks up a tool and demonstrates its use for a particular student. But there is never any doubt that the student "owns" the project and is ultimately responsible for it.

Kids enjoy classes like shop, gym, and band because there's a premium placed on *doing* the activity rather than talking about it. Writing workshop embraces that same premise. Lucy Calkins, director of the Teachers College Reading and Writing Project, has pointed out that the writing workshop is a "generative" time of day, with kids actively involved in creating their own texts. This is important. Most kids experience school as a series of tasks, dittos, assignments, tests—things that are administered *to* them. Writing workshop turns the table and puts kids in charge. This requires us to engage in responsive teaching rather than relying on preset lesson plans.

For some people, the term "workshop" has a laid-back, 1960s, New Age feel that conjures up images of beanbag chairs and a kind of permissive, anything-goes atmosphere. Nothing could be further from the truth. In fact, workshop is a rigorous learning environment that has its roots in the traditional system in which apprentices learned the skills of their trade by working at the sides of master craftsmen and women. The writing workshop puts kids on the spot and makes them responsible for their learning.

If you observe a workshop you will watch a roomful of people engaged in the act of writing. More than anything else, you'll be struck by how much writing kids do. True, teachers often begin by bringing students together for a short lesson, and often end the workshop with some kind of share time. But the core of a workshop—the heart, the marrow—is kids putting words on paper.

Psychologist Mihaly Csikszentmihalyi has described "flow" as the optimal learning condition for human beings. In this state, the learner finds a match between his or her ability and the demands of the task at hand. At that point, the individual enters a "flow zone" in which he or she loses track of time and becomes totally engaged in the task. That's what we're shooting for in the writing workshop. We want to create conditions that allow students to occupy the zone where they can work/play with language, and learn as they do it.

Writing ability, of course, differs from student to student in any given classroom. In a first-grade class, certain kids dazzle you with sophisticated, even literary, writing. For other children in the same class, their writing flow zone mostly consists of drawing pictures, and perhaps labeling one part of the drawing. Rather than setting up a competitive arena, we need to create an environment where students of varying abilities can coexist side by side and learn from one another.

All this might make the writing workshop sound terribly complex and difficult. It's not. It doesn't take long to feel comfortable running this kind of classroom. But it does require a significant teaching shift. The writing workshop does not place the teacher under the bright lights on center stage. Rather, the teacher sets up the structure, allows students plenty of choice, and gets them writing. You work off the energy students create. Yes, there are many moments when the teacher intervenes to teach something. But the emphasis is more on what they are writing than on what you're teaching.

We might clarify our thinking about the writing workshop by considering the conditions present when kids learn other tasks. Take skiing, for instance. Our kids had never skied before. We drove them to the mountain, bought lift tickets, rented equipment, and paid for them to have a lesson. (Ouch!) I can still see our boys standing there, cold and forlorn, waiting for the ski lesson to begin. From their body language it was painfully apparent how uncomfortable and awkward they felt. The lesson began. By midmorning they had mastered snowplowing, and by lunch they had each gone down one of the intermediate trails. We were amazed at how quickly they transformed themselves into skiers. How did it happen? When we looked closer, and reflected on the instructors who worked with our kids, several things stood out:

1. They were all skiers themselves. They wore that ultracool skiing apparel, talked the talk, and radiated contagious enthusiasm for the sport.

2. They believed in *doing* as opposed to *talking*. They didn't begin their lessons with a lecture, ski video, or ski simulator. They helped our kids step into their bindings and immediately got them skiing.

3. They expected plenty of failure. "You're all going to fall a lot today," one of the instructors said with a rueful smile. "Everybody does. You'll probably be pretty sore tonight. But I guarantee you this: by the end of today you'll be skiing."

4. They built on strengths: "You're doing it! You're telling me this is your first time? I can't believe that! You're skiing like a pro!"

The writing workshop strives to create hothouse conditions where our students can thrive as writers. You can see from their body language that many of them lack confidence when it comes to writing. They scrunch down in their seats and cover their papers so nobody else can read them. They feel scared, nervous, inadequate.

We hold those kids in the palms of our hands. We can learn from those ski instructors as we help our students find their stride as writers. We can show them our own enthusiasm for writing, and get them writing on the very first day. We should expect plenty of failure—false starts, blank pages, misspellings, and so on. Failure is an integral part of how people learn. But we also need to build on their strengths—take notice of and celebrate a great word, sudden twist, surprising image—as they shakily get their balance, ease down the mountain, and start making their tracks in the snow.

# The Essentials of
# Time and Space

## 2

Many of us can recall method courses we took during our pre-service teacher education programs. There were courses on reading, math, the sciences, and such. A few of us took a course on teaching writing, though such courses are offered only sporadically at teacher preparation institutes across the country. We probably took a course on discipline and management. It's odd how little attention was given to those two areas that so greatly influence teaching and learning in schools: time and space.

How does our use of time influence what students can and cannot do? How does the physical environment of the classroom affect the way students learn and teachers teach? What do time and space have to do with kids learning to write?

# Time

Through his books and his research, Donald Graves has had a major impact on the teaching of writing. One day a teacher asked Don, "How should I teach writing if I can only sandwich it in one day a week?" "Don't bother," Don replied bluntly. "One day a week will teach them to hate it. They'll never get inside writing."

It is crucial for students to have frequent, predictable time set aside for them to write. Plan to schedule a minimum of three days a week for about an hour each day. Four or five days is even better. It's important that students know when the workshop is scheduled so that they are ready to meet it. When students know they'll have a specific time to return to a piece of writing in progress, they think about that work when they are away from their desks.

When we were in school, most of our teachers randomly assigned writing assignments: "Okay boys and girls. We're going to write today." No wonder it was so hard to get the engine going! And once it did start humming (*if* it did), there was little reason to keep it going. Few of us had the chance to discover what happens when you get into a rhythm of writing regularly.

You may be thinking, with a sense of panic, "Okay, but I don't have three hours a week to spare!" Of course not. Yet many successful writing teachers have found ways to hurdle the time issue. They've done this by scrutinizing their schedules and pruning out other, less effective methods they are using to teach students writing skills. These include discrete language arts lessons, taught in isolation, and writing assignments connected to curriculum but disconnected to one another.

A teacher might say: "But I already do a lot of writing with my students. They keep journals and we work on class writing projects as an extension of our social studies and science units. I also do a big poetry unit every spring that the kids and I love. Do these fit with writers' workshop?"

To answer this question, it's important to carefully consider the purpose of each of these writing activities. Consider journal writing. If you use journal writing mainly as a way to communicate with students (i.e., they write each day, you read and respond), then journal writing serves a purpose other than those met by writing workshop. You may decide to continue using it. But journal writing used this way alone will not develop your students' writing skills.

On the other hand, if your purpose for journal writing focuses on helping students feel comfortable with writing, you may find that journals serve the same purpose as writing workshop. True, journal writing may be more manageable because it keeps the writing in one place and creates a nice history of students' growth. But you could forgo the time devoted to journals and instead have students use writer's notebooks within the writing workshop. The writer's notebook differs from a journal. Encourage students to use the notebook to experiment with writing techniques as well as a place to record important thoughts, feelings, seed ideas, and dreams.

Let's assume you have tackled the time demon and carved out regular class time for the workshop. It's also important for students to plan how they will use *their* time. The wording here is deliberate. When we suggest you schedule time to write, three days a week, we are referring to a workshop environment where student choice is prevalent; where students decide when a piece of writing is finished; where students set their own agendas and their own pace.

Why is choice so important? Let's get right down to it: while the teachers may determine what gets taught, only the student can decide what will be learned. This is true for learners of any age. We learn best when we have a reason that propels us to want to learn.

When students have an authentic purpose for their writing—whether to document an important event in their lives, get classmates to laugh, or communicate a message that matters—they pay attention differently to instruction. Our students know best which topics and purposes for writing matter most to each of them. Letting them choose their own topics and set their own purposes makes it a lot more likely they'll be engaged and receptive.

These are big tasks; students will need our careful attention and coaching to do them well. The structure of the workshop helps teachers provide what young writers need. In the same way that a predictable schedule is important for your students, the regularity of the workshop structure also matters. While individual teachers have added their own rituals and routines, three basic components should be present in your workshop: (1) time for whole-group instruction (often referred to as a minilesson), (2) time for writing, and (3) time for structured response (as a whole class or in small groups). A typical hour broken into these three components is illustrated in Figure 2–1. Let's take a closer look at what the hour entails.

## Minilessons

Of all the workshop components, the minilesson looks closest to what we associate with traditional teaching. Minilessons are short, focused, and direct. The teacher has something to teach, and she gathers together the students to teach it. The topic of the minilesson varies according to the needs of the class, but it typically falls into one of the following categories:

- Procedural (important information about how the workshop runs—how to get or use materials, where to confer with a friend, etc.)

Figure 2–1   Components of an hour-long writing workshop

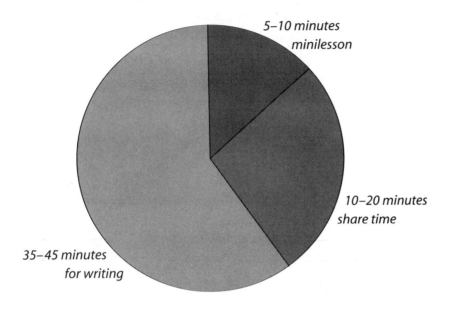

5–10 minutes
minilesson

10–20 minutes
share time

35–45 minutes
for writing

- Writer's process (strategies writers use to help them choose, explore, or organize a topic, cut-and-paste techniques for revising a piece, etc.)
- Qualities of good writing (information to deepen students' understandings of literary techniques: use of the scene, influence of point of view, strong language, leads and endings, etc.)
- Editing skills (information to develop their understanding of spelling, punctuation, and grammatical skills)

The correlation with traditional instruction stops there. A minilesson is not meant to direct the course of action for the rest of the workshop. This is a time to introduce an important skill (for

*The Essentials of Time and Space*          • **11**

example, how strong verbs improve writing), but we shouldn't expect students to spend the next forty minutes practicing it. Rather, teachers use the minilesson to introduce one idea/skill/ strategy that seems relevant and timely for a particular group of writers. Teachers might direct students to practice the skill *during* the minilesson, as with the following instruction: "Choose a page in your writer's notebook and circle the verbs. Can you think of a stronger verb that might replace the ones that you are using?"

But when the minilesson ends, students return to their on-going writing projects, with the focus once again on the goals and intentions they've set out for themselves. It may feel funny to put forth a skill or strategy that your students don't immediately apply in their writing. But you can be sure that such instruction will broaden their visions as writers, and they will bring this broader vision to their work.

## Writing Time

Teachers devote most of the workshop time to actual writing. Beware of having your students spend this time completing teacher-assigned writing projects. This may be considered writing, and may have its own value, but it is not what happens in a writing workshop.

In the first chapter we briefly described the look and feel of the workshop. The room hums with the productive sound of writers at work. During this time, students work on the writing projects they have set out for themselves. Kids are rough drafting, planning, rereading, proofreading, or conferring with other students. Most teachers use this time to move around the room and confer with students as they write. This is the crux of the workshop. We devote Chapter 5 to a close look at the writing conference.

# Share Time

Response occurs throughout the workshop in the form of teacher-student and student-student conferences. But you'll probably also want to schedule a special time for students to share their writing with the whole class. In these share sessions, you coach students in how to give and receive response to each other's writing. Some teachers designate a special Author's Chair for this purpose.

A third-grade boy sitting in the Author's Chair with his classmates around him is getting ready to share a draft he is working on.

"What kind of help do you need from us?" the teacher asks.

Michael shrugs. The truth is, he's not sure what kind of help he needs. That's okay. The teacher has planted the seed of an important idea with that question. Over time your students come to realize that it is helpful when writers direct the kind of response they need.

"Okay, Michael," the teacher says, "would you like to read your piece aloud?"

Michael nods and starts to read:

*I went camping last weekend. We had to hike almost four miles, and by the time we got there I had a blister on my foot as big as a Skittles. First we set up our tents. Then we got a big pile of dry wood for the fire. My dad and the other father took a walk. But when they were gone the wind start blowing. These sparks came shooting out of the fire, and caught onto some dry leaves. Then we had another fire! My friend's big brother, Will, came running up. He was yelling really loud— "Pull that wood back! Move that pile of firewood! Give me that water!" The good thing was he dumped water onto the fire and put it out, but the bad thing was we didn't have much water left to drink.*

"Wow!" the teacher says to Mike. "Does anyone have a comment or a question for Mike?"

"I like when you said your blister was big as a Skittles," one boy says, licking his lips. "I love to eat them!"

"You eat blisters?" one girl asks him. The kids giggle. Michael smiles.

"It must've been scary when the fire started," one girl says.

"Kind've," Michael admits. "After that my dad made a rule that one of the grown-ups had to watch the fire."

As the students respond to Michael, the teacher is listening carefully to see how able they are to confirm what he has done. These kids are doing pretty well.

"Did Will put out both fires with the water?" one boy wants to know.

"No, just the fire in the dry leaves," Michael replies.

"How did he know how to put out the fire?" one girl asks.

"He's a fireman," Michael explains.

"But he's in high school, isn't he?" the girl persists.

"Well, I think he's like a volunteer fireman," Mike tells her.

The girl nods. Her confusion is gone. But this teacher knows that oral clarity is different from clear writing. She decides to intervene and direct the student to look at that part of his draft.

"Michael, you answered those two questions and that cleared up our confusion," the teacher says. "But I want you to go back and take a close look at that part. See if you have written it clearly enough, okay?"

Michael bends forward, rereading his writing.

In this scene we see that share time is for more than just celebrating student writing—it can be a great teaching time, too. Your role in this share session directs students to act in ways that will help them when they are conferring one-on-one with peers. Over time, you'll want to talk explicitly about what makes for good response. The share session gives you a fine opportunity to model it.

The above example describes a whole-class share. Many teachers who work with older students opt for smaller response groups instead. When students begin drafting longer pieces it makes sense to give them steady response partners who can listen more regularly as a piece evolves over time. Of course, students need coaching in this response setting, too. If you begin with whole-group response, you'll find that students can often transfer the skills they learn in the larger setting to this smaller one.

The response group is an example of how you might fine-tune the share. But let's not get ahead of ourselves. For now, it's enough to remember this: kids need regular, predictable time to write. This is as essential as water and light to a plant. They need this time to establish purposes for their writing, and time to achieve those purposes. The more actively engaged students are, the more time you have to coach and instruct them as they grow as writers.

# Space

Space affects us. It invites us to act. Consider how much time we spend creating comfortable spaces where we can do the work we love. Maybe you have a special place in which you like to write—the local corner deli, or the quiet of your office as you curl into an overstuffed chair. We think carefully about the space we need to work, the tools we want at hand, our proximity to or distance from others. We need to bring that same considerate eye to the classroom as we design the space to accommodate the needs of twenty-five or so idiosyncratic writers.

There are certain physical requirements for a writing workshop. We include here the elements that we consider important, and thoughts on each to guide your decision-making process.

## A Meeting Place

You will need a gathering space large enough for your entire class to meet. You'll gather here for minilessons and whole-class response sessions. This might be the spot where you read aloud. It may be a large corner that is set up as a quiet place for students to stretch out on the floor to work. There will be times when you will want to pull students away from their desks to focus on group mini-lessons or individual students as they share their writing.

## A Place for Materials and Tools

Writers, like all craftspeople, need access to their tools. A writer's tools may include:

- Paper, pencils, notebooks, and computers for drafting
- Folders for keeping their work organized
- Scissors, tape, stapler for revising
- Dictionaries, thesauri, word lists, checklists, colored pens for editing
- Trade books for inspiration and technique

Where will these tools be stored? Some teachers establish a Writing Center, where students can go to retrieve necessary supplies. This sounds fancy, though it doesn't have to be more than a small table in the corner of the room, or a cart that can be wheeled to the center of the room during workshop. There will be a steady stream of students coming from and going to this center, so think carefully about where you situate it.

Other teachers bring the materials to their students by placing caddies with most-frequently-used items at the center of student tables. You will find what works for you.

## Carefully Arranged Desks or Tables

There are a number of factors to consider here. First: comfort. We believe people need to be comfortable to do their best work. This means that young writers should have access to spaces in the room other than their own desks. Some students like to write on a clipboard as they stretch out on the floor. Others prefer working at a desk that is pushed off into a quiet corner. Ask your students to think with you about how the space should be used during writing time.

*I wrote about this in my questions!*

Consider your one-to-one conferences. Where will you meet to discuss an individual's writing? While some teachers assign a spot where students come to them, we strongly encourage teachers to go to the students for conferences (stay tuned for Chapter 5). A lot of good teaching takes place in teacher-student conferences. While conferences are designed for a particular student, you will find that nearby students will eavesdrop and also benefit. Cluster desks into groups of four or six so your teaching can spill outside the parameters of a single conference. Clusters of desks also makes it easier for students to ask for and receive help from each other.

Try to envision this space. Place your students in the classroom and watch how they move. Don't forget to put yourself there too. Can you picture yourself conferring with individual writers? Watch as Scott moves from his desk to the Writing Center to get a sheet of paper. Can he move efficiently without having to squeeze through a crowd of desks? Where are the quiet spaces in the room? Where are the places that talk can occur productively? Does the room have enough texture that individual students can find the sort of spaces they need to feel comfortable?

Look on the walls. In one third-grade classroom students can look to the wall of their classroom library to find a reminder of how to choose a topic.

### Where Do Writers Get Ideas?

Rereading their notebooks
Browsing through literature
Talking with a friend
Revisiting old drafts

The best teachers leave traces of their teaching throughout the classroom. This encourages students to continue to practice particular habits of thought. Physical reminders also free the teacher from being the only source of information. Ann Marie Corgill hung this chart in her third-grade classroom, reminding children of the particular ways they can get help from their peers.

### How Can I Help?

Rebecca: trimming the shrubs/sticking to the point
Chelsea: creating believable characters
David Sh: making comparisons/seeing likeness in unlike things
Alice: writing poetry
Meghan: effective leads
Linley: effective endings
John Br: editing for spelling
Robert: giving helpful suggestions/comments

Angela: understanding and explaining the writing rubric
Bradley & Kelly: illustrating
Bobby, John Br. Hurly, Kelly: writing non-fiction with voice
Lydia: using watercolors

Look at the walls again. Is there evidence (student writing, author's quotes, etc.) of the important work that is taking place? When your colleagues come into your room, can they see how you and the students value writing? Can they learn about your students simply by "reading" the room?

The writing workshop is fueled by the unique and boundless energy of your students. Time and space contour the container that will harness that energy.

# *Making It Work*
## *in the Classroom*

▶ Look at your weekly schedule. Find three to five time blocks of fifty minutes or more to devote to writing.

▶ If your schedule appears full to the brim, ask yourself: What lessons or other activities could the writing workshop replace? Are there times already devoted to writing or language work? If so, what purposes do these serve? Might they be better served with writers' workshop?

▶ Let your class know when writers' workshop will be.

▶ Ask your students to talk about what they need in order to make the classroom a comfortable place to write.

▶ Based on this input draw a map of the classroom and share it with them.

▶ In the early weeks of the workshop keep asking the question, "Have we created a comfortable place for writing?" Be willing to make changes along the way as you find what works for you and this particular group of students.

# Short-Term Goals

## 3

Curriculum. It gets written by a group of teachers, inserted into plastic binders, and too often stuck on a forgotten shelf in a corner closet. Which is not to say that curriculum isn't valuable. It can be, especially when it is informed by careful observation of our students. Writing curriculum tends to focus on long-term goals such as:

- writing in a variety of genres: narrative, descriptive, persuasive, etc.
- deepening the connection between reading and writing
- learning the writing process: prewriting, drafting, revising, editing, publishing, etc.
- mastering the conventions of print

Lists of long-term goals tend to be pretty detailed, so much so that your eyes quickly glaze over reading through the pages. Either that or you feel a rising sense of panic as you wonder how on earth anyone could possibly cover so many items.

Before we stress out over long-term writing goals, we have to consider our short-term goals. Our list of short-term goals for the writing workshop is mercifully brief:

- getting students to love writing time
- establishing a safe environment so that kids can take risks in their writing
- setting up a workable management system to handle the flow of paper, folders, and so forth

That's it: three short-term goals. In fact, the first two goals are so entwined you could probably collapse them into one. Students will love to write if they believe they are in a safe place where they can do so.

Many teachers lose themselves in the first month because their eyes get focused too far in the distance. Instead of working on these simple short-term goals, they focus on trying to improve the quality of the writing, or getting students to make substantial revisions. These are appropriate long-term goals, but they will sink the workshop if they become the focal point too early in the year. What are we aiming for in those first few weeks we establish a writing workshop? Let's look at how can we best achieve those short-term goals, one by one.

# Fostering a Love for Writing Time

"We're going to write now," you tell your students. But if they respond by groaning or grumbling, you're in big trouble. You're dead in the water.

How do you make it so your students open their notebooks, pick up markers or pencils, and really want to write? There's no magic answer, and it's a fact that certain kids will stubbornly resist the invitation to write. But it starts by giving them regular time, real choice, and your genuine interest in what they put down on paper.

"Choice leads to voice," literacy consultant John Poeton says when talking about writing. We know that young writers work best when they feel a sense of ownership—personal investment—in their writing. We want them to care about their writing, to have a this-really-matters-to-me feeling as they write.

We touched on the issue of student choice in the last chapter. Choice is not an absolute right, a blank check giving kids a right to write about gruesome, offensive subjects, or subjects that might violate another person's privacy. Still, student choice is the crucial fuel that drives a healthy workshop. And choice isn't limited to deciding what to write about. We invite students to have choice in length, audience, and the pace with which they write.

Don't be surprised when kids decide to write about topics that don't fascinate you. Because their topics are self-generated, the writing workshop truly has a "kid" feel to it. It is flavored by the passions, voices, idiosyncrasies, media influences, and peculiar humor of kids. In a fourth-grade class, you might find one kid feverishly working on "A Most Disgusting Joke Book." Another kid is working on a biography of a professional WWF wrestler.

That's par for the course. When you come right down to it, it can't be *your* writing workshop. If you want it to be alive, truly alive, your kids have to feel that, in the most fundamental sense, the writing workshop belongs to them.

"Do you like to write?" I (Ralph) once asked a fifth-grade boy.

"Yeah," he replied. "'Cept when we have to write for punishment."

"Does that happen often?"

"It happens all the time," the boy said.

"I try to get kids to write about what they know, what's important to them, what they care about," I told him.

"That's our best subject," he replied, nodding.

# Establishing a Safe Environment

When we talk about a safe environment, we mean an atmosphere that encourages kids to take risks in their writing. This might include a boy tackling a sensitive subject, or a girl trying out a new literary technique that will make her writing different from her friends' writing. In many classrooms, students instinctively support each other's writing. But in other cases, you may need to take a more active role in making the workshop a safe writing place. For instance, a third-grade boy reads to the class a poem about his dog, which had recently died. When he finishes, another student mutters, "Oh, how touching," his voice dripping with sarcasm.

Who would want to share personal writing in such a hostile environment? Negative comments like that destroy the feelings of respect and positive support that are so crucial to any classroom community.

Creating a safe environment starts by giving kids choice in what they write. But it doesn't end there. Here are some other ways to foster this kind of environment:

- Give specific praise. You can do so either in a one-to-one writing conference, during the minilesson, or in a group share. When you praise specific elements in their writing—"What a great verb!" or, "That's an amazing lead!"—they begin to open up. After a few weeks they may actually be receptive to your suggestions about how they could improve the piece of writing.

- Let primary children draw. Many students in kindergarten, first and even second grade will spend lots of time drawing pictures during a writing workshop. Lots of teachers get impatient and want to wean kids from these drawings and move them to "real writing." But beware about doing this too early or abruptly. Many kids find drawing to be a safe way to create symbolic representations of what they want to say, what stories they want to tell.

- Read aloud "from-the-heart" pieces of writing. Look for short, powerful texts you can share with your students as models of the kind of writing you're hoping they might do. The poems from *There Was a Place* by Myra Cohn Livingston, for instance, show kids that writers can explore difficult topics. When you read these poems, or a picture book like *Tight Times* by Barbara Shook Hazen in which Daddy loses his job, you show students that strong writing has its roots in the real stuff of life. At the same time, balance this with poems or picture books that show a range of emotions. Students should get the message that they can write about ordinary, everyday events as well as joyful, embarrassing, or poignant moments.

- Use a writer's notebook. Many professionals consider a writer's notebook essential to their process of writing. It is an excellent tool for young writers, as well. Artie Voigt, a literacy consultant in New York, refers to the writer's notebook as a "low-risk, high-comfort" place for students to write. The writer's notebook is a particularly good fit for upper-grade students.

- Write with your students. This may be the most important strategy of all. Nothing creates a supportive writing tone as when you walk in the shoes of a writer yourself. When you take even a few minutes during the workshop for your own writing, you give kids something they rarely see—a real live adult actually writing! Even if writing isn't your strongest suit, you can use your writing as a model for your students. At the same time, you send a powerful message: We're all writers. We're in this together.

# Creating Workable Classroom Management

A writer is somebody who writes a lot. If you tell that to your students, and give them regular time to write, don't be surprised if they hold you to your word. Many young writers rise to the challenge and start producing a great quantity of work. The sheer volume of writing is a nice problem to have, but it can be problematic just the same. It's essential to come up with a workable classroom-management system to handle all the paper that gets generated. Otherwise you'll get swamped.

The crucial word here is "workable." The management system you set up has to work for your students, but it has to work for you too. If it is too cumbersome, complicated, or ambitious, you'll probably end up abandoning it. When it comes to classroom management, every teacher has to devise a system that reflects her or his own personality.

The writing workshop runs best if students can work as independently as possible. If they keep interrupting you whenever they need extra paper, or the stapler, you'll be so distracted you'll never get down to the important work of conferring with your students. You want to set up a "decentralized" classroom-management system. Although there is no single management system that does this, here are a few suggestions for the short-term.

## A Finished Box

Most of us can remember the days when everyone started a writing assignment on the same day and handed it in to the teacher $X$ number of days later. Back then, our teachers thought in terms of "batches" of writing. But the writing workshop recognizes that each writer will proceed at a particular pace, and that this pace may change from one piece of writing to another. You'll want to structure your workshop to incorporate the reality that not all students will be finishing at the same time.

Some teachers use a box or bin and have students place their writing there as they finish it. By using the finished box, a student will not have to interrupt one of your conferences to give a piece of writing to you. The student puts the finished draft into this box, gets some paper, and starts the next piece of writing.

After each writing workshop, or at the end of the day, you will want to empty the finished box and take a close look at the writing you find there. Each of these completed drafts is a real "act of literacy" that will give you a window both into your class and into a particular young writer. You'll notice strengths, weaknesses, surprises. You may notice how short their pieces are, or how much of the writing seems to imitate popular TV shows. You may find rich writing you can use in a minilesson to model a particular technique.

The term "finished" will evolve over time. Early in the year, finished means that the writer is done and has no more to say about the topic. Later, when you introduce a proofreading checklist, you'll teach kids to self-edit a piece of writing before it gets placed in the finished box. Some of these pieces will eventually be read by a larger audience.

## Unfinished Writing Folder

This is a handy folder that you and your students will use in various ways. Students will use it to contain their works in progress. Our friend Martha Horn, a teacher and staff developer, suggests that these unfinished writing folders be color-coded by table, so they can be quickly passed out at the beginning of the workshop and collected at the end of the workshop. Students might create a personalized list of writing ideas, tape it inside the folder, and add to it throughout the year. This form may be as simple as Topics to Write About (see Appendix A), or you could use a form that invites students to brainstorm in a few specific areas (see Appendix B).

Topics to Write About

I am an expert at:

Things I will always remember:

Topics I feel deeply about:

Kinds of writing I would like to try:

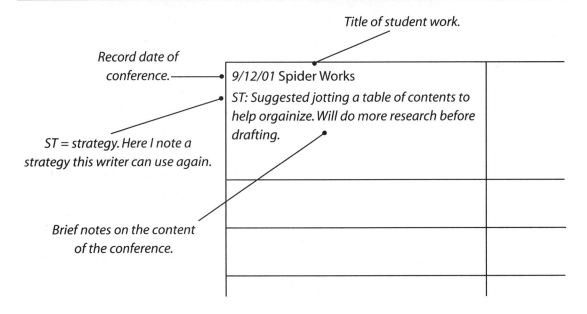

**Figure 3–1  Example entry from Conference Notes form**

*Title of student work.*

*Record date of conference.*

9/12/01 Spider Works

ST: Suggested jotting a table of contents to help orgainize. Will do more research before drafting.

*ST = strategy. Here I note a strategy this writer can use again.*

*Brief notes on the content of the conference.*

Just as a doctor writes notes on a patient's chart, you can use the unfinished folder to keep track of your writing conferences with each student. Use the back of the folder. Jot down the date and the gist of what was discussed (see Appendix C). An example of such an entry is in Figure 3–1.

You might find it helpful to use a sheet that has one column for notes on revision or content conferences and another for conferences that deal with editing skills (see Appendix D).

## Finished Writing Folder

This is a place where each student can file pieces of writing that have been finished. By having a finished writing folder, we are telling students that this writing is important enough to keep together in one place. In some classrooms, kids put a table of contents inside the folder that lists these pieces. It might be a simple list of titles or it could ask students to record what final form the piece of writing took (see Appendix E). A sample completed form is in Figure 3–2. Teachers may also want to use a form to help kids self-evaluate each finished piece. Such a form might ask them to judge their work on a scale of 1 to 5 as in Figure 3–3 (see Appendix F).

While you won't hand out the finished folders at the start of every workshop, make sure students have easy access to them. You may encourage students to go back and reread their finished pieces every so often, and use them as springboards for more writing on the same topic.

There are many other management structures that help the writing workshop to run smoothly. The ones you use should respond to the particular quirks and chemistry of your students. Imagine, for example, that a first-grade teacher has too many students eager to share their writing each day. That teacher could create a simple chart with a list of class members, which is checkmarked after each one shares. Kids understand the concept of fairness and taking turns. A chart like this gives kids a visual reassurance that they'll get their turn in the Author's Chair.

At the beginning of the year, you may devote several minilessons to the particulars of classroom management. These may include how to use the space in the room, the need to return materials to the Writing Center, things to do if you need a conference and the teacher is occupied (find a friend, reread your work seeing if you can solve your own problem, write in your notebook while you are waiting), how to use quiet voices in a peer conference. This is time well spent. After a while, when kids internalize these procedures, they will become second nature to them. Then they can devote all their attention to the work, and play, of the writing itself.

Figure 3–2  Sample of a completed Finished-Folder Contents form

## TABLE OF CONTENTS          FINISHED FOLDER

| DATE | TITLE | Published? If so, how? |
|------|-------|------------------------|
| 9/18 | Sports newscasters | final draft in folder |
| 9/29 | The new Kid who wanted to make friends | Published book |
| 10/3 | Letter for parents night. | Parents liked it. |
| 10/18 | bone book | science fair |
| 11/4 | Hockey Camp | unfinished |
|  |  |  |
|  |  |  |

Figure 3–3  Sample Finished-Folder Self-Evaluation form

| TITLE | NAME Billy Dean | | | | | |
|-------|---|---|---|---|---|---|
| | RATING | | | | | |
| | 1 | 2 | 3 | 4 | 5 | DATE |
| The scariest Thing Ever | | | | | | 9–12 |
| The magic Crystal | | | | | | 9–20 |
| The Sacred Banana | | | | | | 10–1 |
| C. Mills Monkey Cluster | | | | | | 10–22 |
| | | | | | | |
| | | | | | | |
| | | | | | | |
| | | | | | | |
| | | | | | | |

# Making It Work
### in the Classroom

▶ Take a few minutes and list your goals—short and long term—for your students. Keep your lists short and as specific as possible.

▶ Think about how you're going to provide regular opportunities for student choice in the writing workshop.

▶ What steps will you take to help create a "risk-taking environment"?

▶ Think through the flow of the workshop: kids finding unfinished drafts, getting paper, writing, finishing, etc. Do you see any possible snags? What could you do to anticipate those problem areas?

# Launching the Workshop

The writing workshop is such a rich learning environment, you won't want to wait until later in the year to begin. We strongly recommend you start early in the year, as soon as your students' back-to-school heebie-jeebies have calmed down a tad. There's more than one way to launch a writing workshop. In this chapter we'll suggest the simplest approach we know.

## Loosening the Soil

One teacher was surprised the first time she observed a writing workshop. "You mean they just . . . write?" she asked.

Well, yes. But before they actually start writing, you might spend time reading to them. Reading a number of short texts (poems, narrative passages, or picture books) will help "prime the pump" for your student writers. Books like *Fireflies!* by Julie Brinckloe, for example, or Judith Viorst's *The Pain and the Great One* will remind students that real writing has its roots in everyday experiences. (See Appendix G for other suggested books.) Don't get hung up on trying to find brand-new books they've never seen before. If your students already know a book you want to share, so much the better!

After you read these books aloud, you can ask: "Does this book give you an idea you could write about?" This will generate discussion. Students can start their own individual lists of ideas for their writing.

You might also encourage your students to tell personal stories, either to the whole class or a partner. James Britton, whose books have had a seminal influence on current literacy studies, once commented that in a classroom the writing and reading "floats on a sea of talk." Students come to school with a long suit in talking. A typical elementary school student can write only ten or fifteen words per minute, but he or she can speak two or three hundred words per minute! Storytelling takes advantage of this oral fluency.

When students tell stories, they draw on the familiar and can quickly get comfortable with their own voice. Becky Holder, a storyteller in upstate New York, asked a group of first graders if they wanted to tell a story. Those who did raised their hands. Becky used a simple rhyme before calling on the students: "Apple, peaches, pumpkin pie, is it true or is it a lie?" One by one the students sat in the Author's Chair and told a story. When each student was finished, the other kids were asked to extend their fingers if they thought the story was true, or cross their fingers if they thought some part of the story was not true. When kids tell stories out loud to a supportive audience, it won't be long before they are itching to write.

# Surviving the First Day

This is meant as a tongue-in-cheek heading. Survival sounds dramatic, tinged with danger, but you may be surprised to find that it's not as scary as that. In fact, beginning a writing workshop can be a lot of fun. For once you won't have to generate all the content and struggle to teach it to passive learners. The writing workshop puts students on the spot and requires them to be active learners. If it's done right, your students' inexhaustible energy—their stories, interests, passions—will fuel the learning environment.

## The Minilesson

Begin by asking your kids to join you in a meeting area. We often like to start by saying: "A writer is someone who makes decisions: How will you begin? What words will you use? Who do you want to read your writing? How long will it be? Your first decision is—what are you going to write about?" We will return to the idea of writer as decision maker many times in future workshop sessions.

You might start by sharing two or three personal stories from your own life. Keep your stories short. Usually one of your examples will spark ideas for your students to write about. Choose stories with different emotional content—strange, sad, funny. If you tell about the time your cat got run over, you'll likely get twenty-five my-cat-died-too stories!

After you're finished sharing, ask the kids: "Those are my stories. But what are *you* going to write about? Take a minute and think." Then you could say: "Please turn and tell the person beside you what you plan to write about. Don't tell the whole story, just the main idea. If you're not sure, listen to what your partner is going to write about."

Give students a minute or two to exchange their writing ideas. Then ask four or five kids to share their ideas out loud. Being supportive is always important, especially at this crucial moment.

Next, invite students to choose what kind of paper they want to write on. If you provide a variety of paper choices (lined, unlined, large, small, premade books) each student will feel more comfortable as he or she gets started. Now they can begin to write their stories. We tell kids that writing is "chatting on paper."

"Tell me your story," we might say. "I can't wait to read it."

Let them know what to expect: "We'll write for thirty-five minutes, then we'll gather again right back here."

## Writing Time

Find a seat and write with your students. Begin a piece of your own writing, even if you only want to write for five minutes or so. You're giving your students a powerful image: a grown-up doing what they're trying to do. You'll be surprised to see how such a simple thing—writing with your students instead of supervising them—has a remarkable way of setting a serious tone.

After you spend some time writing, you'll probably want to get up and confer with your students. Writing conferences bring you close to the act of student writing. Pull in close. You may want to kneel, sit, or squat so you're at the student's eye level. You'll want to immediately signal that you're in a listening mode: "How's it going?"

Peter Elbow, author of many books on the teaching of writing, once remarked that a good writing teacher is "half-host, half-bouncer"—in other words, both inviting and demanding. Those are two distinct approaches, and they are both important. Early in the year you want to err on the side of being a good host. Many kids already have their writing phobias, and they will drag them into your workshop. The best way to defuse them is by projecting an encouraging, appreciative attitude. Try to be there as a *reader* before you're there as a *corrector*. You've got the entire year to help them polish their writing and refine their technique. Now is the time for you to lavish unconditional support and appreciation.

Keep these conferences short and punchy. Engage, listen, react as a human being. Find something to celebrate in their writing and point it out to them. Then make your exit.

The most predictable problem on the first day: kids with blank papers! Nothing to write about! Expect this problem so you're ready to deal with it. You might interview such students, asking questions to help them find a subject, such as:

- What do you know lots about?
- Do you play sports? What about other activities like dance or chess?
- What number are you in the family? Oldest? Youngest? Middle?
- Who's your best friend? Or a good friend?
- Is there a special relative you spend lots of time with?
- Do you collect stuff?
- Ever go to the hospital?
- Did you ever move? Did you have a best friend you left behind?
- Do you have a pet? Do you wish you had one? What kind?

Ask these questions briskly, without dwelling on any one, and jot down the answers on a sheet of paper. Often kids have a wealth of rich experiences they could draw upon for their writing, but for some reason they censor themselves. When you write them down, they can see all the possibilities. You might suggest: "Read over this list. See if there's one idea that tugs at your sleeve, that makes you want to write about it. I'd suggest you pick an idea where you've got lots to say about it."

A student interview usually works, but it takes up valuable time. You can also help a student by pairing him or her up with another student. Let's say Trey has nothing to write about. You know that Trey's best friend is Josh, so you call Josh over. Use an understanding tone when you explain the situation: "Trey is having a problem that writers have all the time. He's having trouble coming up with something to write about. Josh, don't give Trey a topic, but get him thinking and talking about what he knows lots about. And Trey, you can use Josh as a sounding board to help you figure out what to write about. You guys find a quiet place in the class. Take three or four minutes, and see if you come up with a writing idea for Trey."

By pairing up two writers, you free yourself to meet with other students. And you help kids solve a problem without you. This usually works three out of four times.

Be patient with kids who don't instantly start writing. Certain people take a bit longer to warm up their engines.

## Share Sessions

As you're conferring with students, keep an eye out for writing that you'd like a student to share with the rest of the class. When the writing time is done, ask the kids to stop writing. (Linda Rief, middle school teacher and author of *Seeking Diversity*, asks kids to stop wherever they are in their drafts, even if they're in the middle of a word.) You might inquire: "How many writers are *not* finished? Raise your hands." Usually, most of the kids raise their hands. "I'm not surprised," you can tell them. "It takes time to do good work. We don't want to rush our writing."

Use the last ten or fifteen minutes of workshop for sharing time. Before having the kids reconvene at the meeting area, pick two or three students to share their writing. Only those students should bring their papers to the meeting place. The rest should be empty-handed (no notebooks, pencils, or pens). We talked about sharing time in Chapter 2. But there are special considerations the first time you do this with kids.

The share gives them a real audience for their work. Like many aspects of the workshop, share time seems both simple and complex. On the one hand, it's a time to affirm the work of your writers. The tone should be positive and celebratory. But it must be handled carefully, especially at the beginning, because you are setting a tone for the workshop. Be careful as you select the writing that gets shared early on. When silly, superficial, or offensive writing gets read aloud, other kids are encouraged to produce similar writing. On the other hand, if pure excellence is your main criteria, your weaker writers may feel that they will *never* get to share. On the first day, pick a few kids of differing abilities whose writing models the kind of writing you're hoping other kids will produce.

Kids don't have to be finished with their writing in order to share it with the class. There's two advantages to asking kids to share unfinished work. First, it encourages them to stay with their writing, to revise, and not rush to completion. Also, when you catch young writers in the process of writing they are more likely to see a draft as tentative, not chiseled in stone.

During a share, the student reads a piece out loud. (If it's a long piece, you may suggest a particular page or passage gets read.) Other students listen carefully so they can respond. When the writer has finished reading, ask the class members to respond to questions like these:

- What did you learn from this piece of writing?

- What did this writer do well?
- What questions do you have?

Keep the share positive. When your kids answer these questions, they will tend to talk to *you*: "I like how he described his uncle's fishing boat." Encourage them instead to respond directly to the student writer, or the child sitting in the Author's Chair. After the student writer has received a dose of feedback, you might say: "The class has given you lots of ideas. What are you going to do next with this writing?"

Here's an alternative way to have students share. Instead of putting one student on the spot, you might ask each class member to read aloud one sentence from his or her writing. It could be a favorite sentence, or it could simply be the lead sentence. It's probably best to respond nonverbally at this point, but even so try to project a positive response to each sentence they read. As they each read, and "ante up" a bit of their writing, they break the silence. Next day, or the day after, they might be willing to read aloud their entire draft.

After the first writing workshop only, you might collect the unfinished drafts. Read them over after class, so you can let the kids know you're aware of the range of writing topics.

Take a deep breath. Congratulations: you survived day one!

# Day Two

Begin day two of the writing workshop by bringing your students to the meeting area exactly as you did on day one.

"Remember how yesterday we started with a minilesson before we wrote? We're doing the same thing today. We're going to do that whenever we begin the writing workshop. After we talk, we'll go back and write. And then we'll have our share time."

Early on it's important to reinforce rituals so kids know what to expect. It won't be long before this three-part rhythm—gathering for the minilesson, writing, engaging in share time—becomes second nature to them.

On day two, kids will be finishing up their writing from day one. If you don't prepare for this, you'll have a roomful of students popping up like toasters, yelling, "I'm finished! I'm done!" And you'll be running around the room trying to get them started on their second piece of writing. You can anticipate this situation in your minilesson.

You might say: "Yesterday we talked about the decisions writers need to make. You all decided what to write about. Today you're going to have a new thing to decide. Am I finished? Have I said all that I have to say in my writing? Or do I need to take time to add more?

"How will you make that decision? By rereading what you've written. I'm going to hand back your papers. I want you to read it over and if you've said all you have to say, put the piece of writing in this finished box. If not, continue working on it. When you're done, get going on your next piece of writing." Other strategies for having kids move through this process independently are discussed in the section on classroom management in Chapter 3.

If you are working with young children, you might hold up their work so the class can watch as individual students consider this question of whether they are finished. If you do this, you'll want to start with two or three students who will continue writing. Then send them off to write.

Although writing workshop is not a rigid, rule-based structure, you might begin day two by writing a few simple rules on the board:

1. *Use quiet voices.*

2. *Please don't interrupt.* You can explain that if someone is tapping on your shoulder, it will be hard for you to listen to the person you're conferring with.

3. *Everybody writes.* Student choice is an important component of writing workshop, but it does not include choosing whether or not to write. In gym, everybody gets sweaty. In math, everyone works on math. During writing workshop, everybody writes. That doesn't mean that kids are actually writing down words the whole time. Thinking, rereading, editing, engaging in a peer conference are all part of the package.

In these first two days you've put important rituals in place. A purposeful tone has been set and you've eased the biggest management snag—helping students over the hurdle of what to do when they are done.

Don't be overwhelmed by the amount of writing your students produce. In the early weeks, students can write fast, moving quickly from one topic to another. As the weeks progress, the topics of your minilessons and conferences will give them the help they need to linger longer in a single draft, to return, reread, and revise, to develop bigger projects for themselves. In time your workshop will find a rhythm that feels right for you and your students. In the meantime, appreciate their energy!

# Making It Work
## in the Classroom

▶ Set aside a time where kids can tell personal stories. Structure this time so that each student gets positive feedback (no criticism or specific suggestions) on the story told.

▶ Collect a handful of short stories, picture books, or poems that model everyday-experience writing ideas.

▶ Think of three different stories you might tell your students to get their writing gears moving. The best stories reveal something about you—the time you shoplifted a candy bar and got caught, a terrible haircut you got from your mom, a keepsake given to you by a special aunt. Practice telling these stories aloud, and keeping them short.

▶ Decide what choices of paper you will offer writers.

▶ Set up writing folders for holding works in progress and finished work.

# Conferring with Writers

## 5

Alice is writing about her big brother who just went off to college. Her page-long story describes all the fun things she and her brother do together—roller-skating, getting treats, going to the movies, cooking dinner. Carmen, Alice's third-grade teacher, leans forward.

"Sounds like you've got a terrific brother," Carmen says.

Alice nods, smiling.

"What's your favorite thing to do with him?"

The girl cocks her head, pondering this question.

"Cooking," she says with a big grin.

"Cooking!" Carmen looks surprised. "That's the last thing I expected you to say. How come?"

"Because we love to add things in," Alice explains with a sneaky grin. "Like, extra things that aren't in the recipe!"

"Like what?"

"Well, one time we were making spaghetti sauce, right?" Alice says. "We added a spoonful of peanut butter!"

"Peanut butter? That must have tasted funny!"

"It made it taste better!" Alice insists. "Another time we were making soup, and I told my brother: 'Let's add some mustard.' So we did! Then we added a little salad dressing. It was good!"

"Did you tell your mother?"

"Nope, we keep it a secret," Alice replies.

"I'm wondering if you want to add that to your story," Carmen says. "If you were going to add that part, would it go at the beginning? In the middle? Or at the end?"

"I guess in the middle," Alice says, studying her paper.

"Let's read it over together," the teacher says, "and figure out the best place to add it."

# Conference Fundamentals

The writing conference lies at the heart of the writing workshop. In Australia this has been called the "conference approach" to teaching writing. The writing conference lets you engage in the teaching dynamic that most of us wanted when we entered this profession—a unique one-on-one interaction between you and a student.

When a writing conference works well it is a beautiful thing. You talk with a student, get a dialogue going, make a suggestion, and exit. At its best there's a marvelous kind of tai chi in which you work off the student's own energy, affirming the writer yet slightly redirecting the flow. You may discover that conferring with students feels natural. But don't be surprised if you don't feel comfortable.

As students, most of us had teachers who assigned, corrected, and graded our writing. Many of us never experienced the kind of writing conference we are describing in this chapter. For this reason, conferring with students may feel strained and awkward when you try it yourself. Faced with an expectant young writer, you might find yourself nervously hemming and hawing, wondering, "What on earth am I going to say?" Or you might find that you have so much to say you tend to overwhelm students with suggestions.

Fortunately, conferring with students is a skill that we can all learn. Let's look at some basics you'll need as you begin going one-on-one with the writers in your classroom.

## Listen

We all know the word, but putting it into practice is harder than it sounds. Researcher Dan Lortie has pointed out that about 75 percent of what we do as teachers has to do with what was done to us at the other side of the desk, when we were students. And few of us had teachers who truly listened to us when we were kids. Our thousands of school hours left an indelible imprint: we soaked up the classic school paradigm in which teachers talk and students listen.

The writing workshop directly challenges that idea. It puts kids into an active stance, both when they write and when they confer. This, in turn, requires the teacher to be responsive during a conference. And that starts with deep listening. Every signal we give to the student—leaning forward, eyes alert—reinforces the fact that we have come to listen.

## Be Present as a Reader

Try to react to student writing as you would respond to any other piece of writing you would enjoy reading. Laugh if the piece strikes you as funny. If the writing is sad, make sure the student knows that you feel the sadness. You start by reacting as a human being, and that means bringing your whole heart to the writing conference. Sure, you eventually want to help your kids improve the quality of what they write. But first you have to receive it as a reader. If you want to affect a student, it's important to first let that student see that his writing—its content, what it's about—has affected you.

## Understand the Writer

In a writing conference we mentally "clear the decks" and try hard to understand the writer before us. We're attempting to get a handle on what the student is doing (or trying to do) in the writing, and we draw on our knowledge of the student's history as a writer. During the first half of the writing conference you might ask yourself certain questions that will help you to "read" the student you're working with:

- What can I learn from her body language? Does she seem "up" and engaged, or listless and bored?
- What kind of writing is she attempting? Is it a poem? Fiction story? Personal narrative? Information piece? Notebook entry?
- Where is she in the process? Has she just begun, or is she almost finished?

Once you understand her intention, your goal is to help her achieve it. But you'll also take into account what you have learned about her from all the conferences you've had before. So you continue to ask yourself:

- Is this a genre she has never before tried?
- What are her strengths as a writer?

- What is she ready to learn?
- What surprises me about the student?

You consider all that you know about the student as you decide what direction the conference should take. Often it takes more than a single writing conference to fully understand a student's purpose, process, audience, and so forth. Be patient. Let your understanding develop gradually over time.

## Follow the Student's Energy

If you sit with a kid who is slumped over, cradling her head, that gives you an important clue about how you might proceed in the conference. You might ask the student: "Are you writing about a topic that matters to you? Do you really want to work on this?" If not, you might turn the paper over and suggest that the student pick a topic she finds more engaging. You can't squeeze blood from a stone.

## Build on Strengths

Writers tend to be fragile, highly sensitive, breakable creatures. Student writers aren't always open to suggestions, from us or from their peers. That's why it's so important to give them concrete praise—a wonderful word, sharp image, surprise ending—during the early part of a writing conference. Unfortunately, many of us quickly discover that we are far better at finding errors and weaknesses than we are at locating the parts where the writing actually works well. We may need to unlearn some bad habits. But it's well worth doing so. Most young writers work behind a window of vulnerability that is tightly shut and locked. When you give them specific praise, they open that window a tiny crack.

## Teach One Thing

In a conference there is a natural flow that begins with understanding and moves toward teaching a particular skill, technique, or strategy. These one-to-one encounters are relatively rare in the bustle of classroom life, and they give you a rich opportunity to stretch the writer you're working with. "Teach the writer," Lucy Calkins has written, "not the writing." The idea is to add to the young writer's repertoire of strategies—not merely to improve a particular piece of writing, but to improve *all* the writing that student will do.

# Conference Content

Okay. But what do you teach?

Writing conferences have the same feel no matter how old the students you are working with. But the content changes depending on the age and ability of the student. While most writing conferences are not grade-specific, it's worth mentioning the kind of conferences you might typically see as kids move from kindergarten through middle school.

## Common Writing Conferences in K–1 Classrooms

- *Adding to the drawing*. Primary children often "write" stories using pictures only. We can encourage students to "read" their pictures by asking them to tell more about the story, and then encouraging them to add new details to the drawings. Later, when they are using words to write their stories, they can use this same strategy of rereading and adding details to their written texts.

- *Adding words to a drawing.* In this conference you invite students to add words to go with their pictures. This may involve labeling parts of the drawing, or encouraging the student to write a sentence or two. Taping a pre-cut strip of paper (or a piece of adding machine tape) along the bottom of the drawing provides a space to write about the drawing.

- *Sounding out words.* We might tell the child: "Say the word out loud very slowly. What sounds did you hear? Put down the letters that make those sounds." Important: Ask the *child* to sound out the word instead of doing it for him. If he writes two or three sounds to represent a long word, reread the word and acknowledge the sounds he was able to hear. This encourages independence so he can do it when you're not there. (See Appendix H for further explanation of spelling development and its influence on conferences with emergent spellers.)

- *Using the "two finger rule."* In a kindergarten class, a teacher shows a child how putting a space the size of two fingers between the words she writes will make it easier for her to read back what she has written.

- *Adding more details.* A young writer will often squeeze out a single sentence and, exhausted by the effort, stop. In a conference we might ask: "What else happened?" When the child verbally tells more about the subject, we encourage him to add the information to the writing.

- *Adding a second page (or more).* Many primary kids feel confined to the limitations of a single piece of paper. You can show them how to staple a second page to continue what they are writing.

- *Including a beginning, middle, end.* By drawing on the child's sense of story, we can use familiar language (beginning/middle/end) to suggest another way the student might expand what has been written.

## Common Writing Conferences in Second- Through Fourth-Grade Classrooms

- *Focusing on the most important part.* When kids write "all-about" stories, it often leads to laundry-list writing. In a conference we can ask, "What's the most important part of your story?" and suggest that the student focus the writing on just that part.
- *Focusing when there is more than one story.* Many young writers will glom together two or even three subjects into a single piece of writing. We can help them see that, and show them how each idea deserves to be its own separate piece of writing.
- *Breaking a large topic into manageable "chunks" or chapters.* This is another way to help a student handle a big topic like "Summer Camp" or "My Family." You might start by asking the student to make a simple table of contents.
- *Cutting and taping to add information.* This allows students to incorporate a new section, not at the end but inside the body of writing. In the conference, you can show the student how to reread and decide where the new writing needs to be added. With her permission, you cut open the story at that part and use tape to add a blank piece of paper. This opens up a "window" where more writing can be added.

- *Anticipating readers' questions.* In a one-to-one conference you present yourself as the first outside reader. You can tell the student what you were wondering about, and ask him to consider other readers. What questions might your friends ask if you read your story to them? What information have you left out that they will need?
- *Sharpening a lead.* In this conference we ask the writer, "Have you reread your lead? Does it do the job of grabbing the reader's attention?"

## Common Writing Conferences in Fifth- Through Eighth-Grade Classrooms

- *Using a timeline.* We often suggest that the student put together a quick and simple timeline to mark the important events in a story. "Now, look at your timeline. Where do you think you want to begin? What might you leave out?" This conference could take place while a student is brainstorming, or in the midst of drafting. It helps the writer see new ways to manipulate time.
- *Focusing on the MIT (most important thing).* Many kids skim over the surface of what they're writing about. When we ask: "What's the most important thing in this story?" we invite them to write another draft with this new focus. Sometimes we refer to this as "peeling the onion."
- *Slowing down a "hot spot."* In this conference, we help the student identify the climax or "hot spot" of a story. Then we suggest the student slow this part down so the reader can linger, and not rush through it. The challenge is to take a part of the story that may only be a few sentences long and expand it by adding details, dialogue, or feelings.

- *Selecting authentic details.* The key here is to invite the student to *talk* about the topic, rather than reading and responding to the writing. When you get a student talking about his topic, you will often hear him speak the kind of honest, specific, accurate details that makes writing come alive. Tell those details back to the student, and suggest he incorporate them into the writing if they are not already there.
- *Developing character.* Student writing is notoriously plot-driven. In the conference we can ask the student to slow down and consider whether or not she has spent enough time bringing alive the characters. Here's one way: "Could you take a moment to describe what your grandfather looks like?"

# Conference Strategies

Consider these additional tips on conferring with student writers.

## Keep Conferences Short

Too often we're overly ambitious in a writing conference—we try to do too much. A teacher sits down with a student, reads the whole piece of writing, listens to the student talk about it, points out one or two strong points, finds a particular problem, brainstorms various solutions, and gets a sense of what the student intends to do. As she makes her exit, she glances at the clock and notices that fifteen minutes have gone by!

The fifteen-minute conference is wonderful, but it's a luxury that few teachers can afford. Remember that you don't have to sit while the student decides what to do next. Frame one issue, discuss options, and make your exit.

## Go Beyond What's on the Page

Think back to the conference at the beginning of this chapter. Sparked by her teacher's interest, Alice provided rich additional information about her special relationship with her big brother. This led to an important revision in the writing. Notice that in this conference Carmen didn't limit herself to what Alice had written. Instead, she got Alice talking, and struck a rich vein of gold when Alice started talking about the mischievous way she and her brother cook together.

This isn't unusual. It often happens that the best part of the story has not yet been written down by the student. You've got the best chance to help your student discover those parts if you look up from the paper and get a real dialogue going.

## Get the Student Involved

Students may expect us to evaluate their writing, but in a writing conference we should put this task in the student's lap. One way we can do that is by reading their writing aloud. This gives them the opportunity to hear it in a new way. Instead of waiting for you to react to the writing, the student must now to listen to his words, and evaluate whether or not the sentences do what he wants them to do.

In the best writing conferences, the teacher listens hard and follows the students' lead. You don't want your students to sit passively through writing conferences while you do all the talking. You might conduct a minilesson in which you say: "I can help you be a problem solver in your writing. But it will help me if you are a problem *finder*."

Ask students to reread their writing and put an asterisk next to the place in their text where the writing works well. Ask them to put a circle in the margin next to the place where the writing needs more work. Later, when you confer, you can go straight to the places the student has marked. Even though they may not find the problem/weakness you would identify, you'll want to affirm their attempts at self-evaluating their writing. This marks an important step in getting the student to internalize a sense of what is, and isn't, quality writing. And this can dramatically shorten your conference!

## Know Your Tastes

Writing is not an exact science. Every teacher has a fondness for a particular kind of writing, and it's different for each one of us. Some teachers adore flowery description with rich vocabulary; others love zinger endings or *kapow!* leads. Still others can't resist emotional pieces. Certain teachers favor organization or—let's be honest— neat handwriting above all else. It's important to know your own tendency so you can appreciate those students who may write well in ways that lie beyond the limits of your tastes.

## Tell the "Story of Your Reading"

When I just don't know what to say, I try to simply be a mirror and let the student know what happens to me when I read the writing. I might say: "The piece really grabs me at the beginning when you're getting ready for the camping trip. I love camping! You include lots of great details—I love the part where the only food your friend brought was that giant sausage! Later, right about here . . . when your cousins met you at the parking lot, I got a little confused. There were so many people, and I couldn't tell which ones were your friends, and which ones were your cousins. . . ."

Writing is intensely personal work, and many people have trouble getting outside themselves. Notice that while I'm not telling the writer what to fix, I'm providing an important perspective—the outside reader—that will help him decide if and how to reshape his material.

## Don't Get Into a Power Struggle

Bottom line: the student decides if or when to use the idea you put forth in the conference. Some kids wield this power like a sword, and staunchly resist any suggestions. Try to avoid locking horns with students like that. The challenge is to create the kind of classroom atmosphere where you suggest lots of rich ideas, and students are willing to try them out.

If you are going to confer well with your writers you'll need a generous heart, a long-range perspective, plenty of tact, patience, and stamina. A sense of humor doesn't hurt, either. Remember: there is no "magic conference" when working with a particular student and her writing. Or, to put it another way, you could proceed in many different ways when working with a student and still have a valuable interaction. Be positive. Get the student talking. Don't despair if the student ends the conference with no intention to revise. Good things happen when writers are able to articulate what they are doing and why.

# Making It Work
## in the Classroom

▶ Devise a simple system for keeping track of student conferences. (See Appendix I for one example.)

▶ Practice listening to your students (instead of speaking to them) in a writing conference. Let them speak first.

▶ As you reread your students' writing, practice finding a specific part or passage to praise. Don't forget to point this out to your students.

▶ Try to keep your conferences short. See if you can confer with a total of seven or eight writers during the course of a writers' workshop.

# The Writing Cycle

## 6

When we were in school, our writing teachers tended to value product (finished pieces) over process (how we wrote them). It might seem that by emphasizing process, the writing workshop devalues the finished piece of writing. Not so! No one would deny that the quality of the student's finished writing is enormously important. But the best way to get exemplary writing from our students is by helping each of them find an effective writing process.

The research of Donald Graves and Lucy Calkins demonstrates how even our youngest writers work through a process that roughly corresponds to the cycle of craft professionals follow. While this process could be represented in many ways, the diagram in Figure 6–1 is a good place to start.

This diagram suggests the complexity of the writing process. It's important to recognize that when we talk about the writing process

Figure 6–1 The writing cycle

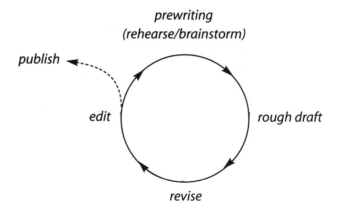

we are *not* describing a "program." Rather, we are trying to reflect as genuinely as possible the cycle writers go through as they write. Looking at a nice neat chart like this, it's easy to forget that each writer is unique. Each writer has his or her own herky-jerky, highly personalized, often ritualized way of getting words onto paper. Any one-size-fits-all writing process would be not only inaccurate but destructive to students.

We don't want to teach our students *the* writing process; rather, we want each one of them to find *a* process that works for him or her. This process will inevitably differ from student to student.

While you can learn from the drawing in Figure 6–1, it doesn't convey the fact that the writing process itself is messy and non-linear. We describe it in separate consecutive stages, but the fact is that writers move fluidly in and out of these stages. For example, a student might be working on a rough draft but suddenly stop to brainstorm the shape of the story being written. And some students will skip one of the stages altogether.

With that important reminder, let's slow down the process and explore the various stages writers go through.

# Prewriting

Many writers consider prewriting an important part of their writing process. Prewriting, also called rehearsal or brainstorming, includes all the cognitive warm-up work that precedes the actual writing. The term sounds formal and intimidating, but that's misleading. Athletes warm up by stretching their muscles; every writer has his or her own way of warming up to the task of writing. Look at this classroom scene:

- Drew is jotting down a list of words in his writer's notebook.
- Alix confers with Rhonda about a story she wants to write.
- David sits on the rug, paging through poetry books, looking for an idea.
- Josh sits at his desk, biting his eraser. There are no words on his paper. He's thinking, planning his story in his head.

All these students are prewriting. There are countless ways of rehearsing for writing. But too often in school the prewriting stage becomes a rigid routine. Instead of kids getting to choose how they want to rehearse for a piece of writing, all students are required to begin by making a cluster web, story map, outline, graphic organizer.

Prewriting should be a help, not a burden, for writers in school. You'll want to show your students various ways they can rehearse their writing. But in the end, let them decide which one, if any, they find most helpful to their particular writing process.

Many young writers use their writer's notebook for the rehearsing, planning, sketching, and wondering that characterizes this early writing stage. With its focus on thinking, dreaming, and gathering, the notebook encourages kids to "live like a writer" during all the hours outside the actual writing workshop. It is important to note that while students do lots of early writing in the notebook, this is an open-ended, generative, playful kind of writing—not the formalized prewriting ordained by a teacher.

# Rough Drafting

Fluency, along with risk taking, is the foundation of a writing workshop. We want to get them moving. Don Murray says that writing should be like riding a bike down a hill, bouncing along, going fast.

But most kids *don't* write very fast. With few exceptions, students have only a fraction of their oral fluency when they write. And when they start looking up words in the dictionary, spell checker, or thesaurus, that meager fluency trickles down to almost nothing. This is frustrating for students. A boy is mentally on the second paragraph of his story, but his hand has written only one sentence.

There are ways to increase writing fluency. Skilled writers learn to separate composing (drafting) from transcription (editing). In a writing workshop we encourage students to concentrate on getting a chunk of text onto the paper. They need to see what the messy rough drafts of professional writers look like. And they should put away editing tools during this stage.

Although we want kids to feel free to compose fluently, this does not mean we should encourage sloppy habits while students are rough drafting. Regie Routman, author of *Invitations* and other books on literacy, points out that it is reasonable to expect even first-grade kids to spell certain words correctly during the drafting stage. We recently worked with one teacher who had replaced the term "sloppy copy" with "best first draft" to describe what she expected from her students during this stage.

# Revising

Read some books on writing process and you might get the idea that kids like nothing better than to revise their writing. Let's be blunt: most kids are not eager to revise. They assume an I've-done-it-and-now-I'm-done-with-it attitude toward their writing. There are several reasons for this. First, they often think of revision as a way to fix a bad piece of writing, when in fact, revision can be a way to enhance a good one. "If I write something that interests me, I go back," the poet William Stafford once said. "If it doesn't interest me, I go on."

We shouldn't force students to revise, but we can show them the alternatives to consider when revising their writing. Here are some revisions I (Ralph) do when I write:

- change the beginning
- change the ending
- add a section (layering)
- delete a part (pruning)
- change the order (resequencing)
- change the genre
- change the point of view
- change the tone

- change the tense
- slow down the "hot spot"
- focus on one part
- break a large piece into chunks or chapters

While students may not do everything that a professional writer can, we can help them expand their repertoire of revision strategies. As you suggest ideas for revision during minilessons, writing conferences, and share time, keep these things in mind:

- Don't expect them to revise everything. The student should decide what aspect or part of the piece to revise. However, it's reasonable for you to expect students to go through the revision process from time to time.

- Make sure they understand the difference between revision and editing. Construct a brick wall between the two! Revision is a composing tool; editing involves the surface features of the writing. If kids confuse the two, their revisions will be first aid (corrections) instead of the radical surgery that leads to improved writing.

- Link revision with what you teach about craft. If you use a picture book to model a strong lead, for example, suggest that students revisit their writing to see if they might sharpen their lead. Whenever you teach kids about writing—details, strong characters, setting—you give them a new way to look at their own writing.

- Model how a particular revision enhanced your own writing. Put a series of drafts on an overhead to show your own revision process to students.

- Be patient. Try not to get frustrated if you don't see as much revision as you'd like. When you're working with young writers, it goes with the territory.

# Proofreading

If the tone is right, your students will feel comfortable enough to share their writing with you and your students in the safety of your workshop. But you should also encourage them to seek a wider audience for their writing. When you publish the writing, you need to make sure the writing will be "reader-friendly," as Nancie Atwell has said. This includes making sure the conventions of language are used correctly. Teachers should not corner the market when it comes to checking for errors. We need to let kids in on the action and help them see when it is appropriate to proofread.

You may want your students to write for three or four weeks without obsessing about spelling and grammar. But at some point you'll want to introduce the idea of proofreading. In Chapter 8 we take a close look at how to teach student writers the editing process.

If you are concerned that kids are not taking editing seriously, take a good look at possible ways for them to publish what they've written. Editing matters when we go from private to public writing. If kids don't have real opportunities to go public, there's no compelling reason for them to proofread their work.

# Publishing

Writing is a form of communication. We write to many different people for a variety of purposes. Some writing is too personal or revealing to be shared. But we want our kids to have the experience of seeing their words fly beyond the confines of their notebooks or finished-writing folders. We want them to see that writing does real work in the real world.

When your kids seek an audience for their writing, do whatever you can to make this experience as authentic and purposeful as possible. During the Persian Gulf War, millions of U.S. children wrote letters to the soldiers in the Middle East. But the purpose and the audience for this writing was determined by teachers. We think it's important for kids to find their own purposes and audiences for their writing. This might include when a student:

- sends a letter to Grandma
- puts together a collection of Grandpa's best war stories
- writes a play and presents it to kids in another class
- writes to a best friend who moved away
- creates a "How to Tame a Baby" brochure with practical tips for kids who want to earn money baby-sitting

Publishing with our youngest writers brings its own challenges. If you're working with primary children, you might think of two kinds of publishing: formal and informal. Formal publishing (involving standardized spelling, grammar, and punctuation) has its place even for kindergarten writers. We don't ask primary writers to recopy their stories. But with your help they can create correctly spelled books that everyone can read.

Expecting the emerging writer to publish with correct spelling and grammar is a little bit like asking a three-year-old to speak perfectly or not at all. One way to honor children's writing is to create classrooms that reflect what they can do. That's why we encourage "informal publishing"—putting students' work up on the wall exactly as they wrote it, with their own drawings, inventive spellings, and so on. It would make sense to see less formal publishing, and lots of informal publishing, in kindergarten and first grade. In second grade the teacher might gradually expect more formal publishing from students.

# The Importance of Rereading

Rereading is the glue that connects the stages of writing. Writers continually reread what they've written, and this rereading changes at each stage of the craft cycle. Picture Chelsea, a fourth grader. After Chelsea has completed the first paragraph or page of her story, she rereads it and asks herself, "Is this any good? Should I be writing this?"

Reading her piece convinces Chelsea that it is pretty good, worth continuing. She keeps writing. After finishing the first draft, Chelsea rereads a second time. This time she asks, "Does this make sense? Have I left anything out? Does my beginning grab my reader?"

Notice that these are big composing questions—not questions about grammar or mechanics—that drive the revision process. Later, Chelsea looks over her story, wondering if she should publish. She decides that she should. Now Chelsea rereads it yet again. This time she looks for errors that involve spelling, punctuation, capitalization, or words she left out.

Rereading is crucial, and too many students don't pay attention to it. If you teach kids nothing about writing all year, teach them how to reread their writing. We tell students, **"You should be the best expert in the world on your own writing, and the way to do that is by rereading it over and over as you write."**

*The Writing Cycle* • **69**

As the year goes on you'll look for different ways to stretch your writers. You'll explore the elements of good writing. You'll move from personal narrative to other genres of writing—nonfiction, poetry, fiction—that will each bring their own challenges. But at the same time you'll continue to explore the writing cycle with students. And you'll try to deepen their understanding of all the moves writers make to bring their words alive.

Helping each student find an effective process of writing should be a crucial part of your writing curriculum. The cycle described in this chapter applies to all kinds of writing. We suggest that you present it to your students not as *here's something brand new* but as *here's something you're already doing in your writing, and I'm going to suggest ways you can do it even better.*

# *Making It Work*
## *in the Classroom*

▶ Begin your own writer's notebook and commit to using it, even if only for ten minutes a day.

▶ Use the thoughts generated in your notebook to develop one piece of writing that you could share with students. Save drafts and revisions to show students.

▶ Reflect on your own writer's process. What are you learning about yourself as a writer that you could share with students?

▶ As you move around the classroom during the writing workshop, pay attention to where each student is in the writing cycle.

▶ Ask students to share their writing processes with the class. Help them become aware of how these processes may differ from student to student.

# Literature in the Writing Workshop

One afternoon last summer I (JoAnn) got caught in a torrential downpour. I had just pulled into the mall parking lot with our son Joseph, seven, who was sitting in the backseat of the car. The rain was thunderous, and hit so fast a large pool formed, flooding two lanes of parking spaces. In the middle of the pool was a drain, creating the most wonderful cyclone of water. It sparked the young boy's imagination. Joseph took one look at it and said, "I know a ghost story." The rain poured down, and I settled in to listen.

"This is a story about a man in a drain who became a skeleton," Joseph said in a low voice. "That's all I know."

"Really?" I asked. "How did he get there?"

Joseph continued telling about a man who went searching for his long lost son. The man came to this very cyclone, peered into the hole, and was pulled down into the drain. After a few more lines Joseph brought the story to a close.

"And every year after that forever and forever whenever someone looks down that drain, they see the skeleton face of the man."

We write with our minds, our hearts, and our ears. Our minds find the topics we know about. They zero in on our expertise and let us know where our knowledge lies. Our hearts guide us to write about the things that matter deeply to us. But what does it mean to write with our ear? When Joseph composed his ghost story, he was composing with his ear. While Joseph's story is short and to the point, he delivered the ending with the knowledge and confidence of someone who knows the sound of a good ghost story. Many of us have students who arrive in our classrooms and, from the very beginning of the year, write with power and passion. Their sense of story is already well honed. Their language sings.

Not surprisingly, these students are usually avid readers. Their heads are filled with stories, poems, picture books, and essays that they have read and reread, and have been read to them. They instinctively know how to linger at the right moment of a story. They craft introductions that take the reader by the hand and lead him deeper into the piece of writing. These students are writing by ear. The ear guides them to emulate the sounds of good writing. How did they learn that? It may be that for these students the sheer presence of good models was enough. But some students need more.

This is where the teacher enters the picture. Good teaching can help all children make the reading-writing connections that certain students have seemingly made on their own. Can you imagine aspiring to be a great chef without having tasted wonderful food? Can you envision becoming an accomplished painter without studying the creative efforts of other painters? How can children improve as writers without ample time spent reading?

But reading what and how? What role does literature play in the writers' workshop? Before we move into literature's place inside the workshop, let's take a minute and consider how the work we do with literature outside the workshop influences what happens within. Most of us read aloud with students, make time for their independent reading, and involve them in some kind of organized book discussions. Let's take a look at how each of these activities nourishes their writing.

# Reading Aloud

Reading aloud builds community. It helps glue the relationships between teacher and students. When I (JoAnn) taught children's literature to undergraduate and graduate students, I often began by asking the students to write a reading autobiography exploring both positive and negative experiences that contributed to the reader they are today. Again and again, students recounted vivid memories of being read to. The students wrote about these memories in ways that suggest that this simple act deepened the bond between them and a teacher. Reading aloud, in many cases, helped them fall in love with a teacher. If you believe, as we do, that relationships greatly influence our students' ability to learn from us and with us, this single factor is reason enough to read aloud regularly to students.

Reading aloud can work magic on a classroom community. It creates common experiences that bind us together. When we share a book like Tony Ross's *Super Dooper Jezebel*, we invite a new character into the classroom. Jezebel is that unlikable child who never does anything wrong. We can talk about how a girl like her makes us feel and how best to react to her edge. When we read books like Eve Bunting's *The Train to Somewhere*, we take a mental field trip to a place and time beyond the classroom. While we might eventually want to study Eve Bunting's craft to see how she detailed the historical setting, for now it's enough that her book lets us experience the orphan trains of the 1800s. Having traveled there together, we are a wiser, more sensitive community.

When we read aloud we learn about our students. Their responses to books open windows into their worlds. Stories beget their stories. Nonfiction titles invite students to bring their own interests into the classroom. Listening to your students' responses to reading provides an intimate glimpse into their lives and loves outside the school and prepares you for moments during the workshop when a student says, "But I don't have anything to write about."

The titles you choose will vary depending on the students you work with. Aliki's memoir, *Marianthe's Story: Spoken Memories/ Painted Words*, encourages immigrant children to share journeys from their homelands and their stories of being the newcomer. Books like David Shannon's *No, David!*, Natasha Tarpley's *I Love My Hair*, and James Stevenson's *I Had a Lot of Wishes* reflect everyday experiences that children share in common.

You'll notice that most of the books cited in this chapter are picture books. Picture books have many advantages that make them ideal for the writing workshop. The brevity of these books allows you to read them in one setting. Since they are so short, they have a lovely transparency that often makes it easier for kids to grasp the elements of writing—lead, setting, shape of the story, climax, ending—than it does when you read a long, complex novel.

For some students, all the reading you do simply adds to the already filled "storehouse" in their heads. But not all children have been read to at home. Not all have had the opportunities to carry such words into school with them. For students who are experiencing literature for the first time, you are helping to build the important foundation they will need to grow as readers and writers.

# Independent Reading

We have four boys, all of whom have passed the early hurdle of learning to read. Each of them has particular likes and dislikes. Our oldest two love fantasy and have been known to reread entire series of their favorite fantasy authors. Although they read a range of genres, they return to this favorite one time and again, seeking new authors as well as revisiting well-loved ones.

Our ten-year-old is still developing his taste. Right now he's more of a book-to-book reader, hopping from one book to another, hoping the new one will be as good as the last. As a younger reader, he had certain picture book writers whose work he knew well and loved. He would choose a book based on the writer's reputation, and could draw connections between a variety of books by a single author, showing us he understood the concept of an author's style.

Joseph, now in second grade, hasn't yet become an independent reader. While he can read, he still prefers to be read to. We do read to him, so he's beginning to develop his taste in books. We'll continue to nurture his independence because we know how necessary this will be as he broadens and deepens that taste.

Regardless of where students are on the road toward reading independence, the time they spend reading books of their choice will fuel their writing. Through independent reading, students discover a genre or author they love. They selectively return to favorites and, through rereading, deepen their knowledge of individual texts. Knowing your students' tastes as readers can help you confer with them on their writing. The authors they love and the texts that have moved them to cry, laugh, or question are the models you will help them to learn from.

# Book Discussions

We read together. We encourage students to develop their tastes as readers through independent reading. We ask students to talk in a lively, free-flowing manner about the books they have read. This may occur during our read-aloud sessions, in small teacher-facilitated groups, or in student-led literature circles. These opportunities increase the number of books you and your students will know in common. Because you and your students have a set of books you know well, you can use these books to talk explicitly about good writing and the many choices writers make as they craft their texts. Here's an example of what that might look like.

A fifth-grade teacher shared Cynthia Rylant's picture book *An Angel for Solomon Singer* during the class read-aloud time. When she finished reading, she invited the students to comment. After a brief discussion she read the book again, this time asking students to interrupt her along the way to share their questions, thoughts, and observations. In this second interactive reading, the discussion helped reveal more of the themes of hope, loneliness, and home that Rylant's work explored.

## Using Literature During a Workshop Minilesson

Listen to how the teacher presented the Rylant book in writing workshop:

> Before you begin your writing today I want us to return to the book we shared last week, *An Angel for Solomon Singer*. Cynthia Rylant uses a technique that many of you might find helpful. Remember when we discovered the illustrator's technique for showing how time was passing? Catalanatto had to move us quickly through time at that part of the story and did so by painting four seasons on one page. He had to move time quickly at that part because Cynthia Rylant moved time quickly in the story. Let's look at how she moved the reader ahead.
>
> (Reading from text): "For many, many nights Solomon Singer made his way west, carrying a dream in his head, each night ordering it up with his supper."
>
> In one short sentence, Rylant makes an entire year pass. This author knows that time doesn't have to move at the same pace. She slowed down the important parts, like the first time Solomon met Angel, and speeded past those parts that didn't need to be detailed.
>
> Some of you are writing narratives, either true or fiction, and there may be places where the reader doesn't need to know everything that happens minute by minute or day by day. You might read your story and ask yourself, where are

the places I can speed ahead? Where are the places I need to move more slowly? If you want to skip time, remember you can do it with a single phrase or sentence. Imagine how each of these phrases helps the writer skip ahead:

Later that day
Every day for the next few months
A week later

Today, before you begin to write, please read over your draft and pay attention to how time is moving in your story. I hope some of you will experiment with moving quickly over a chunk of time. If you do, let me know so you can share with the class at the end of the workshop.

This is an example of a "craft lesson" drawn from a picture book. The book offers many techniques young writers could learn from, but the teacher selected one that seemed appropriate to the needs of her students. She may return to this text at a later date to talk about another writerly technique.

Notice that the teacher drew from a text the students knew well. If the students were hearing this book for the first time, it would be hard to focus their attention on craft. As good readers, they would be busy making sense of what's going on with the story line. Because they spent time doing that prior to this minilesson, they can focus all their attention on the writer's craft.

Here's a list of favorite picture books we have used to teach particular elements of writing.

- *In November* by Cynthia Rylant demonstrates the power of sensory detail and models for students the need to carefully observe the world around them.

- *The True Story of the Three Little Pigs* by Jon Scieszka shows how a story can be told from different points of view.
- *Crow Boy* by Taro Yashima is a great book that shows students several different strategies for making a character come alive.
- *I'm in Charge of Celebrations* by Byrd Baylor and *Tar Beach* by Faith Ringgold each portray a strong sense of place.
- *Charlie Anderson* by Barbara Abercrombie is the perfect book for showing students the power of the surprise ending.
- *Owl Moon* by Jane Yolen is a terrific example of the use of poetic language in telling a story.
- *Dream Weaver* by Jonathan London shows how writers strive to describe the familiar in a fresh new way.
- *Stevie* by John Steptoe helps students learn about voice, and how it can be developed through the use of authentic dialogue.
- *If You Find a Rock* by Peggy Christian gives a fine example of descriptive writing about familiar things.
- *Workshop* by Andrew Clements shows the power of strong verbs.

Literature isn't only used to teach about the writer's craft. Early in the workshop you will find that literature is valuable simply for modeling the possibilities open to writers. We've used books to show how authors can write about the same topic but from the perspective of different genres. Julie Brinckloe's story *Fireflies!* paired with Paul Fleishman's poem *Joyful Noise* and a Let's Read and Find Out book on the same subject can show students how authors choose not only what to write about but also the genre in which they will write. Brinckloe sets out to entertain us with a story and invites us to reminisce about our own experiences. Fleishman's poem is a celebration of language; it helps us see fireflies in a new light (no pun intended!). The Let's Read and Find Out series has the distinct purpose of teaching a subject. This treatment of fireflies educates the reader about everything from flight patterns to how these bugs actually give off their light. Literature can show students that they have choice, not only in selecting a topic but in considering their purposes for writing about a topic.

Literature can also be used to highlight how authors approach the same subject in different ways. For example Mary Lynn Ray's *Mud* and Nancy White Carlstrom's *Raven and River* are two picture books that describe spring. Carlstrom uses a very patterned and detailed approach to describe the coming of spring; Ray focuses on one of spring's characteristic features—mud!

With you as a guide, and literature as the landscape, you can open young writers' eyes to the full range of possibilities before them. Writing asks students to make many decisions along the way:

What will I write about?
What am I trying to accomplish?
How might I begin?
Shall I be playful or serious?
Is this the best word to use here?

Students can't make these choices in a vacuum. Literature fills that void.

# Using Literature in Teacher-Student Conferences

Your individual writing conferences will be enriched by your work with literature as well. Conferences depend on the teacher's skill in bringing out the reader in the writer. As you listen to your students respond to literature, you are listening to the reader in the student. A student who expresses confusion knows that writing needs to be clear. The student who remarks on an author's use of metaphor or description appreciates the visual imagery that writers employ. You want to awaken those reader perspectives during the writing conference. What does that look like? Listen in on the following conference.

TEACHER: Hi David. I see you're still working on your piece about your grandfather's war stories. How's it coming?

DAVID: I'm just finishing the last story and then I'll be done.

TEACHER: Can we talk for a minute? Yesterday when we were reading *The Blue and the Gray*, I noticed you commented on how Eve Bunting kept shifting from the present to the past.

DAVID: Yeah. I thought it was cool the way she put the two stories together.

TEACHER: It seems like you're doing the same thing as Eve Bunting. The story takes place in the present, with you visiting your grandfather. But then you take the reader back to the past when we read about your grandfather's experiences in the war. You could probably get some ideas on how to make these switches between past and present by studying Eve Bunting's book. What do you think?

DAVID: That might help.

TEACHER: Go for it and see what you think. I'll leave Bunting's book here in case you want to refer to it to see what worked for her.

This is one conference unique to this writer and to the reading history of this class. But every workshop is peppered with potential moments like this one. Imagine the teacher as a switchboard operator helping connect particular students with particular texts they know well. The more you know about your students as readers, the better you'll be able to challenge them to think critically about their writing.

We have used literature to help students set writing goals by asking them to think of an author they would like to learn from. What does this author do that you would might want to do in your own writing? Students who read regularly and are encouraged to talk about books from the perspective of writers can rise to the challenge of such a question.

Writing without reading is a little like seesawing alone. Without someone on the other end of the teeter-totter, it's impossible to get off the ground. We don't need literature to get students writing. We can hand them paper and pencils and simply say go. But we need to tap their experience as readers if we really want them to soar.

# *Making It Work*
### *in the Classroom*

▶ Consider your classroom library. Do you have books that can serve as good models for the students you work with? Where will you keep these books so students have ready access to them?

▶ Make a list of twenty picture books you will read aloud (see Appendix G). Make sure five are earmarked for the earliest days and weeks of the writing workshop. Ask yourself: will these books help my students explore topics of their own choice? Do these books model for my students a range of possibilities?

▶ Plan some early activities designed to help you learn about your students as readers: individual surveys, paired interviews, a focused class discussion, a classroom library of students' favorite books.

▶ Design a system for keeping track of students' responses as readers (see Appendix J). Take notes during literature discussions when possible. Use these notes during writing conferences.

# What About Skills?

## 8

(JoAnn) recently returned to skiing after being away from the sport for the last eighteen years. Here's the good news: I find that skiing is a little like riding a bike. I haven't forgotten everything I knew.

But the bad news is that skiing has changed from how it was when I was younger. For one thing, skis are different. The new shaped skis are designed to make it easier to turn. At least that's what everyone says. But I find that my old straight-skiing habits don't work as well on the new skis. "The skis will do the work," friends try to convince me. "Just relax and go with them." I'm listening with a healthy dose of skepticism. I can feel my resistance: "My old skis worked just fine. Why do I need to try something new?" Letting go of the familiar in order to learn something new can leave you feeling inadequate, at least at first.

For some of us, the shift to writing workshop feels like this. The change may ask you to step outside of your comfort zone and trust that you can accomplish old goals in a new and improved manner. Resistance will most likely rear its head around the teaching of skills.

It's hard to argue with giving students regular time to write. Of course they need practice if they are going to get better. But finding ample time for writing means rethinking the way language arts has been taught in the past. Namely, it means no longer devoting the bulk of that time to teaching isolated skill lessons. Can you really teach skills well in the context of writing? Is this really an adequate way for students to learn how to write correctly?

When I first started using a writing workshop, I was concerned that I wouldn't be able to cover all the skills the other teachers on my grade level taught in their more textbook-centered classrooms. What would happen when my students entered fifth grade and returned to the school-wide language arts series? Would they have the skills that other fourth graders had learned? I was a relatively new teacher and this worried me. I didn't want my students to suffer because of my wrongdoing.

I found a compromise. I scheduled writers' workshop for Monday, Wednesday, and Friday, and kept a language arts skill block on the remaining two days. Every Tuesday and Thursday my students and I worked out of the textbook as I selectively taught those lessons that focused on the mechanics of language. Each day my students practiced the new skill in exercises.

Here's what I found. My students could apply these skills correctly in isolation, yet when it came to the workshop they were less likely to use them in the context of their own writing. I found that if I wanted my kids to carry over these skills—which of course is the entire reason for teaching skills in the first place—I needed to embed them in the ongoing life of the workshop. Students needed instruction on the front lines of their writing, and they needed a structure to help them consciously apply these skills.

This realization prompted a new question: What would this embedded-skill teaching look like? More importantly, how would I keep track of what I taught and whether my students were learning?

I sat down with the language arts textbook and made a list of the particular skills that students were expected to know. I was less concerned about composition skills—things like sequencing or developing the main idea—because I knew these skills would be regularly addressed in conferences on drafts in progress. Instead I focused on those skills that dealt with the conventions of language: spelling, punctuation, and grammar. The list fit in a single column down the long edge of an eight-by-ten-and-a-half-inch sheet of paper. I ruled the paper so I had a grid with vertical columns that would allow me to periodically record whether or not individual students were using each skill. I copied enough sheets so I had one for each student and filed them into a three-ring binder. These sheets allowed me to keep track of the skills individual students acquired.

Of course, the chart itself didn't answer my question of what this new embedded teaching would look like. But it was a beginning. I thought of it as my safety net. The chart gave me a way to measure my students' growth. As long as I agreed to use this chart throughout the year as an assessment tool, I could make informed instructional decisions so that students would acquire the skills they needed to learn.

At least four times a year I sat down with my students' writing folders and the checklist to assess their skill development. With a skill such as "uses the correct form of possessive nouns," I would review a student's work and write yes in the box if I saw this skill demonstrated in her writing. If the use was inconsistent, I would mark an S for sometimes. If absent, I would leave the box blank.

*What About Skills?* • **89**

In addition to these regularly scheduled assessments, I informally recorded observations whenever the situation presented itself. For instance, one day I conferred with a student who was using dialogue for the first time. I noticed that he had correctly used quotation marks, and I noted this on his checklist.

When curriculum comes straight out of a textbook, we have the assurance that we've covered the necessary material. But this assurance is misleading, if not false. Yes, you can test these skills in isolation, but that doesn't tell you very much. It's like coaching soccer—sure the kids can trap the ball and kick a goal during practice drills, but can they do it in the game itself? You don't know until you see the kids actually play.

The same thing is true in writing. You watch to see what skills kids put to use in their drafts. Your students' writing—their strengths and shortcomings—determines what skills you will teach and when you will teach them. If you see a need in a single student's work, you can address it in an editing conference. If you notice a lot of students are ready to learn the same skill, teach it during a minilesson.

Let's say that you notice your kids have trouble using commas in their writing. When you teach this skill, talk about it from a writer's perspective. It's important to model not only how to use the comma correctly, but also its purpose. Here's how this might look in a minilesson:

> Writers are always searching for the best way to put words together. Sometimes it's best to use short, to-the-point sentences. Other times you might find that combining sentences is the better way to go. Consider the following example:
>
>> At Disney World we went on Space Mountain. We also went on Thunder Mountain. The Tower of Terror was fun and scary.

There's another way to express this information to the reader. If the attractions mentioned share something in common—perhaps they were all fun and scary—you could combine the three rides into a single sentence and use a second sentence to describe what they were like. Here's a way you could do that.

> At Disney World we went on Space Mountain, Thunder Mountain, and the Tower of Terror. They were all fun and scary.

This second version reads and sounds smoother. Notice how I had to use commas to list the different rides. Whenever you present three or more ideas in a list, you'll need to separate each one with a comma. Some of you may have ideas that could be combined into a list like this. Be on the lookout and if you find some, try combining them into a list in a single sentence.

Minilessons give you a golden opportunity to teach skills like this in short, concentrated bursts, and to connect these skills to the real writing students are doing. Because they are writing on a regular basis, students will respond differently to skill lessons taught in a workshop context.

# Teaching Students the Editing Process

Establishing a clear procedure for editing also helps students develop their skills as proofreaders. Although editing procedures vary from workshop to workshop, there are a few basic steps you will want to incorporate:

1. Create a routine that gives students the responsibility to be their own first editors.

2. Teach them how to implement this routine.

3. Diagnose student needs based on their edited work.

4. In an editing conference, selectively teach one or two skills that students are ready to learn.

Let's take a more detailed look at this process.

## Create an Editing Routine

When we were in school, the students wrote and the teachers corrected. In a workshop, we want students to share the responsibility for correcting work. You'll help students by giving them guidelines on what to look for. Create an editing checklist, and make sure it's not too ambitious (see Appendixes K and L). Three or four skills is plenty. We've seen checklists stretch to two pages long! It would be difficult for anyone to focus on so many skills at one time. The longer the list, the less likely it is that kids will pay attention to it.

The editing checklist you create should reflect the abilities of the students. If the list contains skills that are too sophisticated, it could work against you. For example, if you put spelling on an editing checklist in a first-grade class early in the school year, it could prompt kids to "dumb down" their stories and use only simple words whose spelling they are sure of.

A sample second-grade editing checklist is shown in Figure 8–1.

**Figure 8–1 Sample second-grade editing checklist**

*The date provides a record of the student's growth.*

*Select no more than four skills. These should represent the cutting edge of the student's knowledge. Skills should be within reach but still offer a challenge. Once students begin to use these skills as they draft, replace with a list of more demanding skills.*

Title _____ Name _____
Date _____

| SKILL | Student | Teacher |
|---|---|---|
| I have written complete sentences. | | |
| I have used capital letters at the beginning of sentences. | | |
| I have used correct ending punctuation. | | |
| I have checked for spelling. | | |
| | | |

*The student or teacher may use this blank space to add another skill specific to the writer's needs.*

*Students check off each item as they edit.*

*The teacher records observations about student's editing strengths along with notes on a skill she plans to teach.*

# Teach Students the Editing Routine

Checklists do not teach editing skills. Instead, they give students directions to read in a particular kind of way—by paying attention to the conventions of language. You'll need to show students how to use a checklist. And you'll want to show them how to reread once for each item on the list. It helps to demonstrate the process by putting a piece of writing on the overhead and going through the list, pausing to give students a chance to practice each editing step in their own drafts. This might look like this:

> The first item asks you to check for complete sentences. Read the piece aloud to yourself, beginning at the first word and ending when you come to a period. Pause. Consider. Does that make sense? Is it too long or too short? Make any correction you think is needed. Pick up and begin reading with the next word. When you are done, check off the box and go on to number two.
>
> Next the checklist directs you to check for capital letters at the beginning of sentences. Trace your finger across the page, stopping at each period. Look at the next word. Have you begun the sentence with a capital letter? Continue to the end, checking the box when you are done.
>
> Now, look at each sentence. Read them aloud one at a time, asking yourself whether each is a statement or a question. Does any sentence need the emphasis of an exclamation mark? Check the box and move on to spelling.
>
> Instead of reading sentence by sentence, you can point to each word and ask whether the spelling looks right. (Many professional proofreaders read the piece *backward* to check for spelling errors!) If you find a word that seems to be spelled wrong, underline it.

Some teachers introduce editing to a small group of students as they come to that point in the process of their writing. Other teachers hold off for the first few weeks, letting everyone complete a number of drafts before introducing it to the entire class.

We've had good results asking students to make corrections using a different-colored pen or pencil. You want to see what students are able to find during the editing process. If they make corrections in black pencil, you lose important information. Perhaps a student found twelve spelling errors out of twenty. If the corrections are made in pencil you will more likely notice what the student missed rather than the twelve errors he was able to identify.

Be on the lookout for students who mistakenly think that the fewer errors marked, the better. You can counter this sentiment by letting students know that a well-marked-up text shows the editor was doing a careful job!

## Diagnose Student Needs

Once a student has given editing his or her best shot, it's time for you to step in. If the piece of writing will be published, which means the student will complete a final draft by hand or computer, you will likely want this writing to be fully edited. We think this is particularly true for older students in grades three and higher. But correcting and teaching are two different things. You may play the role of final editor, correcting those errors the student was unable to find. But before you do that, you will want to select one or two skills to teach. To do that, look over the entire piece of writing and ask yourself, "Is there a skill that this piece invites me to teach? Is there something this writer is ready to learn?"

Figure 8–2 is a scene from a story named "Fighting Fruits." Robert wrote this when he was in fourth grade. What do we see

Figure 8–2  Excerpt from Robert's story "Fighting Fruits"

Mechanical MarshMallow uses
a blast from his gun, but
Pear of aces had immproved
Since their last battle
against each other. Pear of aces
Said "I've got an idea I'll
use a bomb that I bought from
a Store. The most fighting food,
Star Fruit, comes in.
Star Fruit is very Stupid,
"Close the door Star fruit"
Pear of aces and Mecnanical
MarshMallow Say.
Suddenly Pear of aces Sees
a letter. He reads it.
It was sent by butter Knife.
He needs Pear of aces for a
fight,
Pear of aces goes to
help But er Knife.
We will finish this later.

   To be continude

here? It's important to begin by noticing what skills Robert can use correctly. He knows to include dialogue inside quotation marks. He's able to use commas to set off a name in the middle of a sentence. He has a good sense of how to write a simple sentence. He understands that proper names require capital letters.

What do his errors teach us? He knows that proper names need capital letters but he's inconsistent in applying this rule and also seems confused when a name stretches across more than one or two words. Notice how he writes the name Pear of Aces as Pear of aces.

He understands that dialogue needs quotation marks, but he doesn't understand how to use the comma to identify who is speaking. It appears he isn't aware of paragraphing at all, either in terms of dialogue or as an organizational tool in writing.

The published version will have all corrections made, but for the editing conference you'll want to select one or two skills to teach Robert. Which shall it be? Since he's showing partial knowledge of the rules of capitalization, it makes sense to start there. Show him how you decide which letters need to be capitalized when a name includes a collection of words. You'll be talking about titles as well since the same rules apply.

Robert is also ready to learn about combining two short sentences into a single sentence. This piece of writing lends itself to that lesson since there are a number of places he could apply the skill. Because he shows an understanding of comma use in a sentence, he's probably ready to expand his knowledge of other ways commas can be used.

## Teaching Skills in an Editing Conference

Let's say you decide to teach Robert how to combine two short sentences into a single sentence. If there were other students who also needed to learn this skill, you could pull them together with Robert for a short, focused lesson. Explain to them what you are going to teach. In this case, you might pick up a pencil and use Robert's draft to show how to combine two short sentences. Then you might hand back the pencil and ask the student to try doing the same thing. Watch closely. When the student seems to understand, let him continue to read his draft and correct for this one particular skill. If this is a new skill, you might ask the student to write it onto the bottom of a new editing checklist and file it away for the next time he edits. This way he'll be asked to continue to work on the skill you've taught as he moves on to his next piece of writing.

This one-to-one skill teaching may seem familiar, and it probably is. But don't get overly ambitious in these editing conferences. It's amazing how fast the eyes of a young writer will glaze over when you start talking about mechanical errors of this sort. Limit yourself to teaching one skill, and, as much as possible, teach it in the context of writing generated in the workshop.

Once I began teaching skills in the context of the writers' workshop, I realized that those out-of-context skill lessons could be cut from my schedule. Eventually, workshop replaced the Tuesday and Thursday language arts lessons, so students were able to write more. More time for writing meant more time for teaching in the manner that worked best—directly related to their own drafts and guided by the skills they needed to accomplish the writing tasks they set for themselves.

# Making It Work
## in the Classroom

▶ Make a list of the language conventions you expect your students to learn by the end of the year.

▶ Create a checklist that students will use to edit their work. (See Appendixes K and L). Select four or five skills most appropriate for your writers to be working on.

▶ Consider how to accommodate the various skill levels in your class. Will there be different colored checklists for different ability levels? Will you use a generic checklist for all students, and leave room where students can add one or two skills specific to their needs?

▶ Consider the materials your students will need to edit their work (colored pencils, word sources, etc.). Where will these materials be kept?

▶ Create a simple way to help you keep track of which individual students have mastered particular skills. (This could be a one page sheet where you can see your whole class at one time.)

# Assessment and Evaluation

**9**

When his oldest brother left for college this year, our son Robert sent him this letter:

*Dear Taylor,*

*Hope you're having fun at Carleton. Is your roommate cool? How's the weather? How are the birds, I mean people, at college? I'm not having fun without you. Tonight Joseph's at Jarod's and Adam's at Cooper's house. The cats miss you a lot—same with me. I'm bored because mom and dad are watching a movie so I have nothing to do. Right now it's 8:23 P.M. on one clock, and 8:25 on the other. Does the food taste good or like pickled pig feet and mustard with mashed potatoes, gravy, and lentil soup blended into a drink with bacon bits on top? I bet it's that second one. It doesn't take a genius to figure out who this is from, but just in case . . .*

*From, Robert*
*P.S. Bring me back a Viking's shirt.*

Putting aside our parents' pride, we would still suggest that this letter shows Robert to be a skilled writer. He has an eye for odd details (one clock says 8:23, the other says 8:25), a sense of humor and play (describing a dinner of mashed potatoes and pig feet for his vegetarian brother), and plenty of voice (you've probably guessed who this is from but just in case . . . From, Robert). He writes confidently to his audience. There is purpose and passion in his words.

A few months later this same writer tore up a letter he had written to an old classmate in Alabama.

"I'm a terrible writer!" Robert moaned.

"What are you talking about?" we asked.

"I only scored sixes on my writing. Everyone scored higher."

"But we think you're a wonderful writer!"

"I am not," he insisted sadly. "I'm a six."

It's true. The year before Robert had written twice to practice prompts, and each time earned a score of six out of a possible twelve. It wasn't that readers didn't appreciate his quirkiness and voice. But these papers had none of the passion you find in this letter to his brother. They didn't show his writing at its best. That's one of the problems with snapshot writing assessments.

But it's more than that. Numbers are like sharp knives; they divide kids into clear-cut categories and numbers that are difficult to forget. The number six sticks in Robert's head. A year later it still casts an indelible shadow onto the image he has of himself as a writer.

Many teachers feel straitjacketed by assessment issues ranging from large-scale tests down to assigning a grade on a student's report card. These evaluation demands differ dramatically from the types of assessments built into a workshop. At first the two might seem to be unlikely bedfellows. We think otherwise. In this chapter we'll look first at the assessments that take place inside the workshop and, later, at how the workshop can flex to address the needs of outside assessments.

# Using Assessment to Inform Your Teaching

In the previous chapter we showed one way to assess student growth in the area of skills. The underlying principles behind that approach hold true for any assessment tool you use in the workshop on a day-to-day basis. To begin, you need a clear understanding of the goals you hold for students. Based on those goals you document your observations of students in action. You reflect on these observations in order to make informed decisions about future instruction.

Sometimes these assessments are quick and easy to implement. Nancie Atwell, founder of the Center for Teaching and Learning in Maine, devised the "Status of the Class," a five-minute roll call during which each student states what he or she is working on for the day. You will find this information highly useful for scheduling that day's writing conferences. "Status of the Class" also gives a glimpse of students' process over time. It may help you to notice that one student writes quickly, jumping from topic to topic without taking time to develop any one of them. You will want to help a student like this learn to read a draft with an intent to revise.

Most teachers create systems for recording what happens in individual conferences. The systems you create will reflect your own organizational style.

We've seen flip charts made by overlapping five-by-eight-inch index cards, one for each student, and taping them onto a clipboard or notebook cover, where the teacher makes anecdotal records about each writing conference. Some teachers prefer to write these notes on the back of student writing folders so students also have a record of what's been talked about (refer to Appendixes C and D). Or they write the notes on address labels clipped to a clipboard, and later file them on individual sheets they have set up for each student in a three-ring notebook.

While these quick and easy assessments are helpful, they don't always do the trick. At certain times you may want to take a slower, more comprehensive look at an individual writer. You can supplement the information you've been collecting by conducting a student interview, or a structured review of a student's writing folder. Appendixes M and N offer guidelines on how to assess growth in primary- and upper-elementary-age writers.

# Getting the Grade

As teacher, you will have a rich and complex understanding of the writers in your class. Suddenly the outside world wants a peek. You can invite a parent in and show her this complex view, but you can't avoid the fact that in other instances you will be required to boil this information down into a single grade. And it's hard to avoid the times when your students will be evaluated on the basis of a single performance. How does the workshop prepare you or them for these forms of assessment?

"What about grades?" a novice workshop teacher asks. "Do I assign a grade on every paper?"

We don't believe in grading everything that students write. In elementary classrooms we suggest not assigning grades to individual papers. Instead, base your grade on the body of a student's work.

Here's why. Students need to take risks to develop as writers. You'll want to encourage them to try new genres and experiment with different literary techniques. Remember that ski instructor who warned the kids, "You're going to fall a lot today." When writers are taking risks, they "fall" a lot, too. That attempt at humor may not work the way they had hoped. The first go at creating a scene with dialogue might sound stilted. Would assigning a grade to such endeavors help the student? We don't think so.

There's another danger. Putting a grade on top of a paper often erases the student's own evaluation of the work. As teachers, we should not be the only voice when it comes to assessing the quality of a piece of writing. We want students to evaluate their work as well. This keeps them growing as writers. Students can self-evaluate informally during a writing conference. Encourage this talk by asking evaluative questions:

- Can you tell me about something you did particularly well in this piece of writing?
- How does this piece compare to others you have written recently?

- Is there something you are proud about doing here?
- Is there any place you are less than fully pleased with?

Older students can write their evaluative comments, which then become part of their writing record over the course of the year. (See Appendix O for one possible form.)

This does *not* mean that you step out of the role of evaluator. If you feel you must grade papers, grade them selectively. Ask students to submit a certain number of completed pieces to be graded during each marking period. This allows them to submit the writing that represents their best work. They can still take plenty of risks and not be penalized for the falls. Ask them to submit a self-evaluation along with the writing. You can place your evaluation alongside theirs and use this as a basis for discussion. Students benefit from our judgment when it is tied to specific criteria that students understand. If you are going to grade, talk with students ahead of time about what you look for in an A paper, a B paper, and so on. Put this information in writing in the form of a rubric, and ask students to use it when evaluating their work.

Some teachers feel fine about not giving letter grades for papers, yet are still required to submit a grade on report cards each time a marking period closes. What then? It's true that the workshop doesn't generate letter or numerical grades in the same way spelling or math does. With these subjects, several grades can easily be averaged into a single, objective one. An overall grade in writers' workshop usually comes from a combination of factors you have identified as critical. These might include:

- *Quality of composition.* Your specific criteria will vary depending on the age of your students but may take into consideration questions like the following: How well written is the student's work? Is the information presented clearly? Does she develop her points with enough detail? Does the order flow smoothly? Is her use of language effective and engaging?

- *Correctness of conventions.* The concern here is on the surface features that make the writing decipherable to readers. Again, make sure your expectations are age-appropriate: How able is the student to apply the rules of written English? Is he able to edit and correct for spelling? Does he routinely use correct punctuation and grammar?

- *Use of a variety of composing and revising strategies.* Does this student fully engage in the writing process? Does she try the strategies presented during minilessons and conferences for exploring a topic before writing or for improving on a written draft? Does she regularly reread her work and think about how to make it better?

- *Participation in the workshop.* Is the student a contributing member of the workshop, offering helpful comments to his peers during share sessions and one-on-one conferences? Does he use his own time wisely?

You arrive at grades by reviewing student writing folders. In a writing folder you can see how much work a student produced, the range of genres and topics explored, the kinds of revisions attempted. You can evaluate the quality of work in terms of vocabulary and description, content and mechanics. You often have anecdotal records to complement the student's own writing. (Remember all those notes you took during writing conferences?) Taken together these documents provide more than enough evidence to assign and justify a grade.

Keep in mind that the students are an important audience for this kind of assessment. Involve them in the process as much as possible. I (JoAnn) asked my fourth-grade students to review their writing folders each quarter and to write about what they saw. They each conducted an inventory of their work (see Appendix P), counting the number of finished pieces as well as those they may have started but then abandoned. They reflected on what they saw as their best accomplishments and they set goals for the writers they wanted to become. As coevaluators, they listened differently to the assessments I offered in return.

# Statewide Writing Tests and the Workshop

Surely, these two can't be compatible! Writers' workshop honors student choice, unlimited time, the response of a supportive reader. None of those elements are present in statewide writing tests that require students to write to a prompt in a specified amount of time without the benefit of an outside reader.

It's true that the testing situation varies dramatically from the workshop environment. Let's return to our skiing metaphor to explore the relationship between the two. Imagine it is a couple of years down the road, and some of those beginning skiers have decided to enter a race. They know that winning the race will depend on one performance down the raceway. They will have to bring all they have learned about skiing to this single moment and this single course. What will contribute to their ability to ski in top performance on that day?

They will need to know the course. It will help if they each have a chance to take some trial runs. They'll hope for the best conditions—to be well rested, well fed, confident. And they'll want good snow! But none of these will matter if the skier hasn't had something else—lots and lots and lots of time to ski all over the mountain. Some of it just for fun; other times with a ski instructor by their side.

Writing workshop is that mountain. Your students need time to write their hearts out; to explore many different subjects; to write deeply about a single one. They need to write for the fun of it, and at times they need coaches by their sides stretching them to write with more precision and craft.

It boils down to this: Your students will perform fine on these tests so long as you provide them with regular opportunities for writing in the workshop.

Sure, writing during the workshop feels different from writing during a test. Still, when we look at the two side by side (see Figure 9–1) we see that the workshop gives students the chance to develop skills they'll need to use independently when it's time to take the test.

The workshop gives students choice over topic and pacing, allowing them to seek help from both written resources and their peers and teacher whenever they need it. The testing situation doesn't allow for any of those. But consider this: Students who write regularly learn about their own writing processes. They know whether it takes them longer to generate ideas or to refine those thoughts once on the paper. Because they have regular experience with editing, they know how long that process usually takes them.

Students who write regularly develop the habit of rereading their own work. Because they have worked in a setting that allows peer and teacher response, they often have internalized the questions

Figure 9–1  Overlap between workshop and test environments

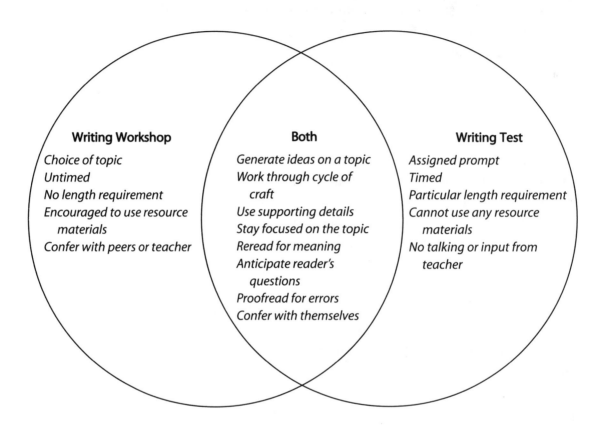

**Writing Workshop**

*Choice of topic*
*Untimed*
*No length requirement*
*Encouraged to use resource
   materials*
*Confer with peers or teacher*

**Both**

*Generate ideas on a topic*
*Work through cycle of
   craft*
*Use supporting details*
*Stay focused on the topic*
*Reread for meaning*
*Anticipate reader's
   questions*
*Proofread for errors*
*Confer with themselves*

**Writing Test**

*Assigned prompt*
*Timed*
*Particular length requirement*
*Cannot use any resource
   materials*
*No talking or input from
   teacher*

a reader will ask. They can call on this "internal reader" during the testing situation. There are specific things we need to do during the workshop to help foster the independence students will need for the testing situation.

- Encourage students to be problem finders as well as problem solvers. What's not working for you here? What do you think the problem is? How could you solve it?
- When they finish a piece of writing, ask them to reflect on the process that worked for them. Ask them to talk about problems they may have encountered and how they solved them. Encourage them to identify the strategies they used that worked. Ask the questions: What are you learning about yourself as a writer? What do you know about the process you use that helps you write well?
- Don't let peer conferences interfere with students' own rereading. Encourage students to spend equal time rereading their own work imagining they were reading it to the class. What would your classmates say? Teaching them to have a conference with themselves gives them practice using their internal readers.

Students will still need coaching on how to put to use all they've learned in the writing workshop. It's a good idea, of course, to give students practice with the testing situation. You may want to share the Venn diagram in Figure 9–1 and talk with students about how they can use what they know about writing in this new situation. Before handing out the writing prompt, give students the following pointers:

- Think about the prompt and identify the kind of writing being asked for. Does the test ask you to write a story, persuasive piece, explanation, or a descriptive paragraph?
- Once you've identified the kind of writing, think about what you know about how to write well in that area. For example, stories require engaging leads, developed character, a developed beginning, clear plotline, a satisfying ending. Explanations require

concise language and a clear sequence. Strong description draws on the use of all senses and the poetic elements of language.

- Use prewriting strategies you have found helpful to uncover what you know and feel about the topic.
- After you have written a draft, have a conference with yourself. What questions would a reader ask? Make revisions as needed.
- Once you are satisfied with the content, turn your attention to editing. Make corrections by reading carefully and slowly using the process we use during writing workshop.

After students have written, ask them to reflect on the following questions: How did you feel taking this test? Did you pace yourself well? If not, what do you need to adjust? Were there places where you got stuck? What strategies could you use to solve this problem during the actual test?

For better and for worse, statewide writing tests are a reality for teachers—and for students. If students are to score well on these tests, writing instruction has to include more than teaching the rules of language and grammar. It has to include attention to composing itself. Students need to spend time writing, to develop successful processes for writing, and to learn to recognize quality both in terms of meaning and skill. The workshop gives them the opportunity to do all of these things.

# Making It Work
## in the Classroom

▶ Decide how you will assign quarterly grades for writing (if you are required to do so).

▶ Ask yourself what information you would need when it comes time to assign grades.

▶ Design some simple systems for collecting that information throughout the quarter.

▶ Devise a way your kids can be involved in self-assessing their writing (see Appendix O).

# Troubleshooting

## 10

The writing workshop does not always run as smoothly as we might like. Like weeds in a garden, certain problems will show up from time to time. Unless you are very lucky, you will run into your share of them. In Chapter 4 we explored ways to deal with those students who sit at their desks with blank papers in front of them when everyone else is writing. In this chapter we'll troubleshoot several other predictable problems, what causes them, and what you can do to root them from your garden (or at least learn to live with them).

## When the Writing Workshop Is Too Noisy

Most writing workshops have an audible hum. In one corner of the room you are softly conferring with one student. Meanwhile the other kids are writing, reading aloud their drafts, giving each other suggestions, getting up to get the stapler, looking for the thesaurus, and so forth. To a large extent, the tone during your workshop will reflect your own preferences and teaching style. Some teachers can tolerate a surprising amount of chatter during the writing workshop; others try to create a library-like silence. Bottom line: The workshop should be as quiet as you need it to be. If it's too noisy or chaotic, you'll be too distracted to confer with your students.

If your writing workshop is too noisy, look below the surface to see what is causing the noise. In other words, look at noise as a symptom of a deeper issue. What might that issue be? It could be that kids don't know what to do when they're finished with a piece of writing. In this case, you'll want to devote several minilessons to the procedures of the workshop: what students should do when they're finished, how to use the finished box, where to get more paper if they should need it. If kids don't understand the flow of the workshop, and have not internalized the guidelines you set up, they will create distractions each time they finish a story or poem.

If your students are noisy, it could also be a sign that they're not writing about meaningful topics that matter to them. In that case, you'll want to stop to address this issue through a minilesson.

## When You're Not Happy with What Kids Are Writing About

Kids choose their topics in the writers' workshop. But sometimes what they write about (silly, violent, or offensive subjects) can make us very uncomfortable. What to do?

Let's begin by acknowledging that there will be a built-in culture clash in the writing workshop between our adult world and the world of our students. Tom Newkirk, author and professor at the University of New Hampshire, has written revealingly about this clash. He points out, for instance, that although we might tend to use works of literature as models for young writers, it's more likely that kids will draw their inspiration from pop culture—rap music, action films, TV shows.

Keep this in mind as you look at your students' topics. We shouldn't encourage kids to be silly when they write, but we should try to understand why they are doing it. Kids are drawn to the zany, silly, subversive humor of writers like Dav Pilkey or Jon Scieszka. It's also important to recognize that writers grow by experimenting, pushing themselves, taking risks, trying something new. We may not always approve of their writing experiments, but it's important to remember that they are playing with the power of writing when they explore material that is adult, violent, or dangerous.

That still leaves us with the question, How do you handle this kind of writing? First, it's up to you to clearly state the boundaries for what kids write about and what language is permissible. You can use the issue of audience to frame this issue: "There are students in this class who will be offended if you choose to write about something sexual, or gruesomely violent. I will be, too. I don't think it's appropriate in school. For that reason, I'm going to ask you to refrain from writing about these topics."

If kids spend four or five hours each day playing video games, it should not surprise us when these kids want to write Nintendo stories. Many teachers discourage this kind of writing, as they do the retelling of TV shows or movies. One teacher told her students: "I could rent that video and find out about it. But in your writing, I want to hear *your* ideas, read *your* original creations."

When you see this kind of writing, ask yourself, What is the real-world writing the student is trying to do? In one class, two boys kept retelling movies they had seen, complete with dialogue. The teacher asked the boys if they had ever seen a film script. They had not. She went to the library and got the scripts for two children's books that had been made into movies (*Matilda* and *Indian in the Cupboard*). Fascinated, the boys read over the scripts. Later, the teacher brought the video of *Indian in the Cupboard*. The boys followed the scripts as they watched the movies. The boys ended up writing their own script for a movie they wanted to make.

## When Kids Use Inappropriate Language

This one is tricky. We don't want to see our students' stories peppered with curse words. But when students use idioms, slang, local dialect, even grammatically incorrect sentences (particularly in dialogue), it often contributes to the authentic voice in the writing. Try to be diplomatic in these situations. We know one teacher who told her students: "It's okay to use the language of the playground, but I don't want to see the language of the street. I don't want to see four-letter words in your writing." This seems like a reasonable compromise. Most (though not all) kids are adept at "code-switching"; they are sensitive to the fact that what is appropriate in one context may be inappropriate in another.

## When Kids Finish Pieces Too Quickly

Both in school and out, our kids live in a fast-paced, hurry-up-and-move-to-the-next-thing world. With its emphasis on taking the time and care to craft writing, the writing workshop goes against this current. No wonder students have trouble slowing down so they can linger in their stories and make them come alive in the fullest sense of the word. If you run into this problem, here are a few things to consider:

1. Make sure you aren't emphasizing that each student must have a certain number of finished pieces. If you are, students will be racing to see who has the biggest stack of writing.

2. Don't make it a requirement that kids can only share finished pieces with the whole class.

3. Let primary kids draw pictures. Drawing will make them dwell in the story, and will often encourage them to go back and add more words.

4. Let students know you're paying attention: "I notice that you pick a topic and finish it in half a page. My goal for you is to find the kind of topic you can sink your teeth into, write a whole page on, maybe even two pages. Let's think about how you could do that."

## When Kids Don't Finish What They Start

As Donald Murray says, "Many writers can begin, but few can close." It's important that students can begin a piece of writing, work through its challenges, and bring closure to it.

Consider first the issue of time. Ask yourself, Am I giving my kids regular, sustained time (at least three times per week) in a writing workshop setting? If many of your students abandon stories they have started, that could be a sign that your students aren't getting enough regular, sustained time to write. If a student starts a piece on Monday and doesn't return to it until the following week, it is likely she will lose interest in it.

The source of this problem may also be topic choice. If they are not writing about topics that matter to them, they won't feel the desire to finish.

## When Students' Writing Is Flat and Dull

Often you see a kind of bare-bones student writing that is nothing more than a plot summary. We call this the *Dragnet* syndrome: "Just the facts, ma'am." When this happens, you'll want to help kids write the kind of sentences that lift off the page into the imagination of their readers. The best way to address this problem is to tap books with lyrical language, such as

*The Borning Room* by Paul Fleischman
*Owl Moon* (picture book) by Jane Yolen
*The Scarecrow* (picture book) by Cynthia Rylant

Read these books out loud to your class. Ask your students, "What sentences stuck in your head?" You might talk with your students about a "golden line"—a sentence or phrase that will stay in the reader's mind for a long time. Challenge your students: "Do you think you could write a golden line? Could you describe something familiar in a brand-new way?"

Flat, dull writing might also be a sign that you need to spend more time in minilessons teaching the elements of good writing.

Also, you might consider tapping into their oral storytelling strengths. You could also set up a structure where your students tell their stories to each other. Listen in on these tellings and write down the particular way students describe a person, place, feeling, or event. You may be struck by the difference between what students say and how they write. Describe this difference to your students, and repeat some of the things you heard them say when they told their stories. You might remind them that writing is talking on paper. Challenge them to bring some of the freshness of their oral tellings into their writing.

## When You Don't Know What to Teach in a Minilesson

The minilesson is an opportunity to give students a focused burst of writing instruction. But when it comes to writing, many teachers run out of things to teach.

As you read through your students' writing—both finished and unfinished—you'll notice where their writing needs improvement. That's where your minilessons come from. Let's say you notice that nearly all your students' stories begin "One day" or "One time." Bingo: you'll want to do a minilesson showing them different kinds of leads they could use to begin a piece of writing. Here are some other ideas for minilessons:

1. Procedures/classroom management. The minilesson is a time to remind kids what to do during the workshop.

2. Celebrate kids' writing. Use this time to read selections from the writers in your class. Find examples of good writing that other students might learn from. Never use a piece of student writing to illustrate a weakness.

3. Read a short passage from a picture book or chapter book. Ask students, "What makes this writing work so well? Is there something that this author does that you could borrow and use for your own writing?"

4. Share your own writing. You'll find it very helpful to share writing that you're struggling with.

Don't get obsessed with the minilesson. It's not absolutely necessary to have a minilesson at the beginning of every writing workshop. You may decide to begin by getting your kids writing. In this case, the share time may be the place where you teach about writing.

## When You're Overwhelmed by Student Conferences

One teacher put it this way: "When I move around the room during writing time there is a 'tail' following me, a tail made up of all the kids who want my help!"

In a class where many kids have their hands in the air, asking for you to confer with them, that's a sign that the kids don't feel independent enough to work on their own. "Good writing teachers find a way to put themselves out of a job," Lucy Calkins has said. If students insist on bringing you in on every writing move or decision they make, they will eat you alive.

When this happens you could stop the class and address the problem directly. You could remind students that writers are decision makers. Tell your students: "Don't sit there waiting for me to come to conference with you. It's up to you—what are *you* going to decide to do? Keep writing. I'll get to you when I get to you." It's important to give students a clear signal to solve their own writing problems— even though they may not solve them the way you would want!

## When Student Editing Is Haphazard

Troubleshoot this common problem in three ways. First, make sure you've got some kind of editing checklist, and make sure it's not too long. Four items on the checklist are plenty.

Second, make sure students are rereading the piece each time for a particular skill. It doesn't work very well if they are only rereading the piece once and trying to find errors in capitalization, punctuation, and spelling during a single reading.

Finally, and most important, consider whether your kids have regular opportunities to go public with their writing. If they don't get to publish some of what they write, there's no compelling reason for them to focus on making that writing "reader friendly."

## When the Workshop Energy Runs Low

You often see this problem later in the year. The kids seem to be running out of steam. And they act like they have nothing left to write about. There is a natural ebb and flow to a writing workshop. Don't be surprised if your class gets a case of the writing blahs every once in a while. Here are two possible solutions.

When the energy runs low, it might be a great time for a genre study. In other words, it might be time to move the kids from personal narrative to a new kind of writing: poetry or nonfiction, for instance. Many students seem to sleepwalk through personal narratives but suddenly perk up when we challenge them to write poetry, or try their hand at information writing. Now you can bring new books as models into the writing workshop. Your minilessons will have a new focus, too. If you're doing a genre study on poetry, your minilessons will focus on metaphor, line breaks, white spaces, and so on. Writing in a new genre usually breathes new energy into the workshop.

You might also rejuice your workshop by having a big splashy Author's Day celebration. This gives them a chance to revisit all that they've written and get it ready to be read by the wider public. An Author's Day will create a lot of excitement; we suggest you schedule one not at the end of the school year but in the middle, so you can reinvest the energy it creates back into your writing workshop.

## When Too Many (or None) Want to Share

You often see this problem with primary children. At the end of writing time, every kid has a hand in the air, waving madly, begging to share a story. It's hard for so many kids to sit quietly while one child gets to sit in the Author Chair. We suggest you reserve share time for two or three students. But once in a while you might want to break the class into small groups of three or four. While this doesn't give students the whole-class spotlight, they at least get the satisfaction of reading a story to another person. This satisfies the writer's need to have his or her words heard.

With older writers, you often see the problem in reverse: *nobody* wants to share. This happens for many reasons. For one thing, preadolescent kids become more self-conscious and private. They're often not eager to make themselves vulnerable and share their inner selves with peers. Also, by sixth or eighth grade, kids know who the outstanding writers are in the class. The other kids may have already ceded over this territory. Setting up small-group shares or pairing one student with another is a good way to handle this problem.

## When Kids Don't Want to Revise

Reread the section on revision in Chapter 6. In addition, Ralph Fletcher has two good books to read aloud to students—*Live Writing* and *How Writers Work*, especially the chapter "Revision: Radical Surgery." These will spark revisions.

Let your students choose which pieces they want to revise. Don't expect them to revise everything.

Be patient. As you become a more skilled writing teacher, you learn the hard truth that kids don't always write the way the textbooks tell us they should. Despite our best efforts, kids will produce a lot of goofy, fluffy, zany, sketchy, sentimental, first-and-only-draft writing. All of that seems to be a necessary part of their writing development.

# Yearlong Horizons

**11**

Planning for the writers' workshop offers particular challenges for the teacher. On a day-to-day basis, the writing workshop requires a responsive kind of teaching. You select topics for minilessons for tomorrow based on what you see your students doing today. The lessons learned in conferences are closely connected to what each student needs at the moment. This may seem uncomfortably spontaneous, but the truth is that skilled writing teachers are also guided by a sense of where they are headed and the goals they aim to accomplish. They hold in mind the image of a year's writing curriculum as they make daily or weekly decisions.

We've looked at the moment-by-moment, day-to-day intricacies of the workshop. Now let's stand back and take a broader look, envisioning one possible timeline for how the workshop might proceed from the beginning of the school year to the end. Of course, there isn't a single right way to plan a yearlong writers' workshop. You will find your own pace, and your own areas to focus on, connected to your particular curricular and setting demands. What does hold true across grade levels and contexts is the need to conceive the year in seasons, with a series of closures and new beginnings, pauses for reflection, and challenges to spur growth. As you read the following sequence, imagine how you might design a framework tailored for you and your students.

# Timeline for the **Year**

### August  Set the Tone

* Who are we as readers and writers? Spend the early weeks learning about each other and building the risk-free environment students will need to grow as writers.
* Emphasis in the workshop is on helping students find topics that are meaningful. Older students might be working in writer's notebooks only.
* Focus on putting workshop routines into place.

### September  Time to Celebrate

* By the end of the first month, make sure that all students have published at least one piece of writing. Keep this simple! This may mean sending visiting authors out to read to other classes. Or you might emphasize finding the natural audience. (Ask students: "Who would you like to have read this piece?")
* By now you've introduced the editing process to older students (grade 3 and above), and students have begun experimenting with simple revision strategies.

### October   Time to Pause

* Take time out of the workshop for students to reflect on the writing they have done during the first term of the school year.
* Students use this reflection time to establish goals for themselves over the next term. Encourage goals that help them deepen their knowledge of the processes that work for them.

### November  Stretch Your Writers

* Weeks 10–17 offer a great time to introduce new challenges to the class. This may come in the form of a genre study where time is spent focusing on the qualities of writing specific to one kind of writing: poetry, picture book writing, fiction.
* Introducing formal publishing provides a new challenge for K–2 students. It develops their sense of audience and raises expectations for the quality of their work.
* With older students make sure clear expectations are established to be used as criteria for grades.

### December  Establish Closure

* Culminate genre study in a celebration of finished work.
* Set time once again for reflection. Ask students to assess themselves against earlier goals they set. Make time for setting new goals.

## January    Begin the Year Anew

- Find a tangible way to signal that January is a time for new beginnings. This may mean brand-new writing folders, clean record-keeping charts, a clear bulletin board awaiting students' words.
- Revisit workshop routines and procedures with your students. Ask them: "Are there changes that would make our workshop better?"
- Have students generate writing of their choice and spend time reading and discussing quality literature.

## February    Transform into a Research Workshop

- Now that students understand the routines of working independently, using teacher and peer response, you can apply these same skills to the research process. Use the workshop—its structure, routine, and emphasis on doing—to coach students in researching and writing about nonfiction topics.
- Set a date to present finished work with others in the school and/or community. Be creative: Create a wax museum, put on a teaching fair, have students display what they have learned through bulletin boards.

## March    Time to Pause

- The end of the third term invites students to reflect once again on their growth over the year. Use self-evaluation conferences to discuss your observations of each student's accomplishments and collaborate on setting goals.
- Use this reflection to launch a focus on revision. Invite older students to return to an earlier piece of writing. Discuss revision as a process of re-seeing. Ask students to recast the topic in a new way: What can you do today with this topic that you were unable to do two or four months ago?
- Make time for students to learn from each other's processes. Again, find a way to share and celebrate work with others.

## April    Reap the Benefits

- At this point in the year you know your students well. And students have found their strides as writers. Use your conferences to help students set challenges for themselves in the areas where they succeed: Do you love to write poetry? Use your skills as a reader and let other poets challenge you to new heights.
- Continue publishing.
- Three weeks before the writing test date, give students practice runs writing to a prompt.

## May/June    Look Ahead

- Time to clean house.
- As students gather their work from the year, spend time thinking about the place writing will have in their lives outside of school and in the school years beyond.
- What have you learned about yourself as a writer that you will use in the future? How will you use this knowledge at home or in a new school setting?

# A Few Last Words . . .

Recently we rode a ski lift with our second-grade son, Joseph, and his first-grade friend, Cody. Amid their chitchat, this exchange took place.

CODY:  There's a boy in my class . . . ? Well, he just learned to put a period at the end of a sentence, so now if the sentence ends with a question mark or an exclamation point he, like, still puts a period!

JOSEPH (amazed):  He puts a question mark *and* a period, too? He puts them both?

CODY (agreeing):  I know!

In this book we have explored a lot of topics: minilessons, revision, conferring, skills, evaluation, planning. They are all important, but they sometimes cloud the issue. A chapter titled "Trouble-shooting" might lead you to believe that running a writing workshop is akin to ridding your hard drive of computer viruses. It's not. We should never forget that the central kernel of our work is not writing but real kids—their voices, passions, imagination, their original slant on the world.

There is a place for a book like this one—and many others we would recommend for writing teachers—but ultimately our teaching must be guided by our students. Listen to them. Watch them write. Try to figure out what blocks their writing fluency. Watch where the class energy falters or soars. Be flexible enough to revise your own teaching to respond to the needs of these novice writers. Pay close attention to the "language stories" like the one we tell here; they have worlds to teach us about the way kids learn about language.

In *The Blood Flows Like a River Through My Dreams*, Nasdijj talks about writing: "I know nothing about the technical stuff of writing or where to put a comma. . . . What I know about writing has to do with where you put your heart."

Nasdijj's words resonate with our own task as writing teachers. In the long run, what will matter to your students probably has less to do with the tips and techniques you show them than with your passion for writing, and your faith in them as writers. If through your workshop they come to believe in themselves as writers, you will have given them a gift that will sustain them for years to come.

# Topics to Write About

| I am an expert at: | Things I will always remember: |
|---|---|
| Topics I feel deeply about: | Kinds of writing I would like to try: |

| Conference Notes | | |
|---|---|---|
| | | |
| | | |
| | | |
| | | |
| | | |
| | | |

# Writing Conference

| CONTENT AND REVISION | EDITING SKILL |
|---|---|
| | |
| | |
| | |
| | |
| | |
| | |
| | |
| | |
| | |
| | |

| TABLE OF CONTENTS | | FINISHED FOLDER |
|---|---|---|
| DATE | TITLE | Published? If so, how? |
|  |  |  |
|  |  |  |
|  |  |  |
|  |  |  |
|  |  |  |
|  |  |  |
|  |  |  |
|  |  |  |
|  |  |  |
|  |  |  |
|  |  |  |

| NAME_____ | RATING | | | | | |
|---|---|---|---|---|---|---|
| TITLE | 1 | 2 | 3 | 4 | 5 | DATE |
| | | | | | | |
| | | | | | | |
| | | | | | | |
| | | | | | | |
| | | | | | | |
| | | | | | | |
| | | | | | | |
| | | | | | | |
| | | | | | | |
| | | | | | | |
| | | | | | | |

# Books to Read Early in the Year

### Books for Getting to Know One Another

The early weeks of the school year are about building community. A good way to get to know one another is by telling stories. And one of the best ways to elicit those stories is through good literature. The following books invite rich conversations and can leave a class feeling closer.

| | |
|---|---|
| *I Had a Lot of Wishes* | James Stevenson |
| *No, David!* | David Shannon |
| *Painted Words Spoken Memories* | Aliki |
| *The Relatives Came* | Cynthia Rylant |

### Books to Trigger Ideas

We look for books that model, in a simple way, the kinds of writing children might do themselves. These books seem so doable, students will think, "I could have written that!"

| | |
|---|---|
| *One of Three* | Angela Johnson |
| *My Bike* | Donna Jakob |
| *City Street* and *Nature Walk* | Douglas Florian |
| *My Mom Travels a Lot* | Caroline Feller Bauer |

### Books That Model Possibilities

The following books show students how to write from their personal experiences and expertise in a variety of ways.

| | |
|---|---|
| *My Map Book* | Sara Fanelli |
| *Bugs* | Nancy Winslow Parker |
| *Learning to Swim in Swaziland: A Child's Eye View of a Southern African Country* | Nila K. Leigh |
| *If You Find a Rock* | Peggy Christian |

### Books That Model Your Passion for Reading

Only you know which books you absolutely love! It's important to include these when you read aloud to your students. Your love of reading will influence the way they feel about reading.

# Strategies for Teaching Spelling

| Stage of spelling development | Strategies to use in conferences |
| --- | --- |
| **Precommunicative**<br>In addition to drawings, the student uses a variety of symbols in place of letters to represent meaning (scribbles, invented letters, etc.). | • If drawings aren't present, ask student to "read" his work and encourage him to add pictures.<br>• If drawings are present, ask students to describe what is happening in the pictures.<br>• Select parts of the picture and encourage labeling with emphasis on initial consonant sounds to teach or reinforce letter names and symbol representation. |
| **Semiphonetic**<br>Students use the consonants they hear at the beginning and/or ending of words, sometimes including middle consonants. Inclusion of vowels tends to be rare. | • Encourage students to sound words out slowly, reminding them that they may need to say the word more than once. Ask students: What do you hear first? What do you hear next?<br>• May encourage finger spacing between words.<br>• Encourage students to read back what they have written, pointing to each word. |
| **Phonetic**<br>Student uses consonants and vowels to represent all the sound sequences he hears. | • At this stage, student work is usually intelligible to author and reader. Continue to encourage risk taking by responding to the meaning of the text rather than drawing attention to incomplete spellings. |

(continued)

| Stage of spelling development | Strategies to use in conferences |
|---|---|
| | • Continue to provide strategies to help student flesh out words. (Using rhyming words, or other known words that sound alike.)<br>• Begin to teach common spelling patterns (-ing) and high-frequency sight words.<br>• May ask students to proofread for a select group of known words. |
| **Transitional**<br>Writers begin to move away from only using phonetics and begin to use visual cues and meaning-based units of spelling (e.g., past tense is usually represented by -ed). Students typically stay in this stage for a long period of time (possibly several years). | • Encourage student to attempt all spelling.<br>• Have students proofread by identifying words that don't "look right."<br>• Encourage multiple strategies for correcting spelling. (Try some alternative spellings, use of class word lists, wall stories, dictionaries.)<br>• Establish the expectation that spelling be corrected when writing is published. |
| **Correct**<br>Entire words are most commonly spelled correctly. | • Students regularly proofread all work.<br>• Continue to stress the importance of correct spelling on all published writing. |

Adapted from *Ideas for Spelling*, by Faye Bolton and Diane Snowball, Portsmouth, NH: Heinemann, 1993.

# Daily Record Sheet

| NAME | Mon. | Tues. | Wed. | Thurs. | Fri. |
|------|------|-------|------|--------|------|
|      |      |       |      |        |      |
|      |      |       |      |        |      |
|      |      |       |      |        |      |
|      |      |       |      |        |      |
|      |      |       |      |        |      |
|      |      |       |      |        |      |
|      |      |       |      |        |      |
|      |      |       |      |        |      |
|      |      |       |      |        |      |
|      |      |       |      |        |      |
|      |      |       |      |        |      |
|      |      |       |      |        |      |

TITLE _____

| Notes on Read-Aloud Response | Possible Minilessons |
| --- | --- |
| | |

# Editing Checklist

TITLE _____    NAME _____
DATE _____

| SKILL | Student | Teacher |
|-------|---------|---------|
|       |         |         |
|       |         |         |
|       |         |         |
|       |         |         |
|       |         |         |

# Skills to Include on an Editing Checklist

This list suggests a range of editing skills. Select *three or four* at a time. Aim for skills that represent the just-right level for your students—those that are not too easy or too hard.

## Primary Writers

Did I write my name and date?

Have I given my piece a title?

Have I reread, pointing to each word?

Can I hear any more sounds?

Can I add any words I may have left out?

Did I begin each sentence with a capital letter?

Did I end each sentence with a period?

Did I use capital letters in all the important words of the title?

Did I underline three words I'd like to see the correct spelling of?

## Elementary Writers

Have I used capital letters for the names of specific people or places?

Did I end each sentence with the proper punctuation: . ! ?

Have I fixed sentences that are strung together with the phrase *and then*?

Am I using the comma for lists?

Have I circled the words that look wrong?

Have I underlined incorrect words and found the correct spellings?

Have I used quotation marks to show when people are speaking?

Did I get rid of any unnecessary words?

## Intermediate Writers

It is important to move beyond the basics with older writers and show them how editing can fine-tune their writing in more sophisticated ways.

Have I used commas for compound sentences?

Have I correctly written dialogue in paragraph form?

Have I indented paragraphs when needed?

Have I avoided passive tense whenever possible?

Have I varied the pace of sentences to get the effect I want?

Have I pruned out the small words that qualify how I feel and think (a little, sort of, kind of, quite, pretty much, in a very real sense)?

Have I cut clutter and tightened my writing by using precise language?

Have I chosen strong verbs?

Have I used contractions when appropriate to bring a more natural voice to the writing?

# Assessing Growth in Primary Writers

Read through a collection of the student's work and consider the following:

1. What does the writing reveal about the writer's knowledge of language? Make a list of all this writer knows. Be expansive.

2. What risks does this child take as a writer?
   - Does writer take risks with spelling or is writing limited to those words student can spell correctly?
   - Does student manipulate the paper by adding or taking away pages to fit the needs of the story or does the paper determine the length of the writing?

3. What patterns emerge as you read through the writer's work?
   - Is there a sameness to topics/purposes?
   - Does student use paper in similar ways?
   - Is there a formula applied over and over again?
   - Is there a recurring theme in the texts or drawings?

4. What changes have occurred over time? When arranged chronologically, are there changes in:
   - the spelling?
   - the quality or length of each text?
   - the drawing or use of paper?
   - the relationship between the drawing and the text?

5. Does student have a clear strength as a writer? This could emerge in the writer's knowledge of conventions, in the quality of composition, or in the process the student employs.

6. Based on your observations, what is this writer ready to learn next? What instruction might the writer benefit from today? What experiences or situations might be fruitful for future growth?

# Assessing Growth in Elementary and Intermediate Writers

1. Ask these questions as you reflect on the student's process:
   - How does the student use his/her writing time? How does the student use others—peers and teachers?
   - How would you describe this writer's process? What works particularly well for the writer; is there anything that hinders his/her process?
   - What risks do you see this student taking as a writer?

2. Study a portfolio of this student's work. In reviewing it consider this:
   - the types of writing the student has attempted
   - the type and quality of revisions present
   - the quality of the finished product, both in terms of craft and conventions

3. List the student's strengths:
   - as a composer
   - as a reviser
   - as a conference partner
   - as a speller

   What concerns, if any, do you have in each of these areas?

4. Involve the student in self-assessment and goal setting. Sit together with the portfolio and ask the student to talk about how he or she has grown as a writer this year. Try any or all of the following. Ask student to compare an early piece with one written more recently. Ask student to select and talk about what makes this his or her "best" work. Ask student to talk about a piece of writing that failed and what lessons the experience taught. Finally, encourage the student to set one or two goals to work toward.

5. Spend time gathering your thoughts from all the above. Think about the goals you would set for this writer and what you might do to encourage growth in that direction.

# Self-Evaluation Form

TITLE _____ NAME _____ DATE _____

What do you think you did particularly well in this piece of writing?




What do you think is the best part of this piece? Why is this the best?




If you were to work on this piece to make it better, what could you do?




Did you learn anything while writing this that you can use in the future?

_____ QUARTERLY INVENTORY    NAME _____

How many pieces of writing have you completed this term? _____

How many pieces of writing did you begin and then abandon? _____

What different kinds of writing did you try?

What was the biggest success you had this quarter with your writing?

What was the biggest problem you encountered? How did you solve it?

What have you learned about your writing process that will help you as you continue to write?

What is something you cannot do now that you would like to learn to do in your writing next quarter?

What goals (name 2 or 3) will you set for yourself?

# Glossary

**Audience:**   The reader or readers of a particular piece of writing.

**Authentic purpose:**   A reason to write connected to an author's desire to do "real" work in the world within or beyond the classroom.

**Author's Chair:**   A designated place in the classroom where the writer sits when sharing with the class. Sharing from the Author's Chair usually signifies a particular form of response (e.g., help for work in progress, celebratory comments for finished work).

**Assessment:**   Ongoing means of monitoring students' work and progress. Results used to inform teaching decisions.

**Craft lesson:**   A minilesson designed to focus on one specific quality of good writing.

**Composing strategies:**   Tools or techniques writers use to successfully complete writing. These include strategies for prewriting, drafting, and revising.

**Conventions of language:** Language conventions reflect current social usage for spelling, grammar, and punctuation; in other words, the way in which we communicate — spell, punctuate, and structure our language — is governed by socially sanctioned patterns of usage.

**Drafting:** The fluent, tentative writing produced early in the process, when the writer's focus is on content and meaning.

**Editing:** The process of rereading a text and correcting mechanical errors according to the standard conventions of language.

**Editing checklist:** A guide that directs students to edit their writing for particular skills, and supports them in doing so.

**Generative curriculum:** The portion of curriculum that is determined based on the current needs and interests of the students at hand.

**Genre:** A particular type or category of writing. The variety of genres students produce may include memoir, poetry, nonfiction, realistic fiction, recipes, biography, fantasy, comic books, and movie or book reviews.

**Lead:** The opening of a piece of writing. It may vary in length from one sentence to several paragraphs, sets the tone for the piece to come, and is designed to keep the reader reading on.

**Minilesson:** A short, focused lesson, often at the beginning of the workshop, designed to address an issue relevant to the community of writers in the classroom.

**Personal narrative:** A story told from first-person perspective. Usually true.

**Publish:**   The point at which a piece of writing is presented to an audience other than the writer. This includes both written and oral means of presentation. Formally published written work usually means the writer has carefully edited the work and presents an error-free finished draft.

**Prewriting:**   Also referred to as rehearsal or brainstorming, this involves writing, talking, or thinking that is generative, open-ended, and meant to help a writer plan for the writing to come. Like all aspects of the writing cycle, this is a highly personalized process varying according to the writer and the specific task at hand.

**Prompt:**   An assignment that directs students to generate a particular kind of writing (usually narrative, descriptive, expository, or persuasive) on a particular topic.

**Peer conference:**   A conversation during which a student seeks response to his or her writing from a peer in the class.

**Reading-writing connection:**   An internal connection students make when they begin to read with the eye of a writer and write with the eye of a reader. Teachers can strengthen this connection by offering opportunities for students to pay attention to writer's craft in the books they read and to shift from writer to reader when working on their own drafts.

**Response group:**   A small group of students who meet together over a period of time to give each other response to work in progress.

**Revision:**   The part of the writing cycle where students reread and make meaning-based changes in an earlier draft in order to clarify, develop, or sharpen their writing.

**Rubric:**   An assessment tool that clearly states the standards to which a piece of writing must be held in order to receive a specific evaluation. Used by both students and teachers to develop common language and understandings in order to evaluate writing.

**Share session:**   A time when the entire class gathers, preferably away from individual desks, to listen and give response to a writer.

**Voice:**   The particular way a writer chooses to "speak" on paper. We say that writing has voice when we can hear the writer directly behind the words.

**Writer's craft:**   Techniques or elements of good writing used by writers to produce quality work.

**Writing cycle:**   The process through which a writer works to produce a finished draft. Includes rehearsal, drafting, revision, editing, publishing.

**Writer's notebook:**   A blank book used specifically to think about and develop one's skills as a writer. A writer's notebook is typically used to collect ideas for writing and about writing and to experiment with writing techniques in a risk-free manner.

# Twelve Books for Tomorrow

There are many terrific books available for teachers who want to expand their horizons as writing teachers. These books are a great place to go from here.

Anderson, Carl. 2000. *How's It Going?* Portsmouth, NH: Heinemann.
*In readable, anecdotal prose, Carl Anderson explores the writing conference and shows concrete ways to become more skillful when responding to writers.*

Atwell, Nancie. 1998. *In the Middle.* Portsmouth, NH: Boynton-Cook.
*Atwell's book transformed middle schools across America. This is a must read for anyone working with middle school and junior high writers.*

Calkins, Lucy. 1994. *The Art of Teaching Writing*. 2nd ed. Portsmouth, NH: Heinemann.
*This comprehensive book is an invaluable resource for anyone who wants to delve deeper into the particulars of the writing workshop.*

Fletcher, Ralph. 1993. *What a Writer Needs*. Portsmouth, NH: Heinemann.
*This readable book has been used at writing projects around the country to help teachers acquire a deeper, more profound understanding of writing and how to teach it.*

Graves, Donald. 1994. *A Fresh Look at Writing*. Portsmouth, NH: Heinemann.
*A great book to share with a study circle. Graves suggests "actions" to take that help teachers look closely at their students, their classrooms, and their teaching.*

Harwayne, Shelley. 2001. *Writing Through Childhood: Rethinking Process and Product*. Portsmouth, NH: Heinemann.
*This breakthrough book covers a whole range of subjects including the reading-writing connection and helping students keep a writer's notebook.*

Heard, Georgia. 1989. *For the Good of the Earth and the Sun*. Portsmouth, NH: Heinemann
*In this thoughtful book, Georgia puts forth a way to teach poetry that is organic and deeply respectful of children.*

Hindley, Joanne. 1996. *In the Company of Children*. York, ME: Stenhouse.
*Hindley writes about her multiage third- and fourth-grade class-*

*room in this comprehensive guide for running parallel reading and writing workshops.*

Rief, Linda. 1991. *Seeking Diversity.* Portsmouth, NH: Heinemann.
*Like Atwell's, this book shows how writing workshop happens with middle school kids.*

Wood Ray, Katie. 1999. *Wondrous Words.* Urbana, IL: NCTE.
*A practical, yet lyrical book about teaching students how to learn from other writers.*

Wood Ray, Katie. 2001. *The Writing Workshop: Working Through the Hard Parts (and They're All Hard Parts).* Urbana, IL: NCTE.
*A brand-new book that covers all the important bases of workshop teaching written in Wood Ray's lyrical prose.*

Zinsser, William. 1994. *On Writing Well.* 5th ed. San Francisco: HarperCollins.
*A great book that reminds us of the power in clean, unadorned writing.*

# Books Cited

Abercrombie, Barbara. 1995. *Charlie Anderson*. Illustrated by Mark Graham. New York: Aladdin Books.

Aliki. 1998. *Marianthe's Story: Spoken Memories/Painted Words*. New York: Greenwillow.

Banks, Lynne Reid. 1985. *Indian in the Cupboard*. New York: Doubleday.

Baylor, Byrd. 1986. *I'm in Charge of Celebrations*. Illustrated by Peter Parnall. New York: Atheneum.

Brinckloe, Julie. 1986. *Fireflies!* New York: Aladdin Books.

Bunting, Eve. 1996. *The Blue and the Gray*. Illustrated by Ned Bittinger. New York: Scholastic Trade.

———. 1996. *The Train to Somewhere*. Illustrated by Ronald Himler. New York: Clarion Books.

Carlstrom, Nancy White. 1997. *Raven and River*. Illustrated by Jon V. Zyle. New York: Little, Brown.

Christian, Peggy. 2000. *If You Find a Rock*. Illustrated by Barbara H. Lember. San Diego, CA: Harcourt Brace.

Clements, Andrew. 1999. *Workshop*. Illustrated by David Wisniewski. New York: Houghton Mifflin.

Dahl, Roald. 1988. *Matilda*. Illustrated by Quentin Blake. New York: Viking.

Elbow, Peter. 1998. *Writing with Power: Techniques for Mastering the Writing Process*. New York: Oxford University Press.

Fleischman, Paul. 1993. *The Borning Room*. New York: Harper-Trophy.

———. 1992. *Joyful Noise: Poems for Two Voices*. Illustrated by Eric Beddows. New York: HarperCollins.

Fletcher, Ralph. 2000. *How Writers Work*. New York: HarperCollins.

———. 1999. *Live Writing*. New York: HarperCollins.

Hazen, Barbara Shook. 1983. *Tight Times*. Illustrated by Trina Schart Hyman. New York: Viking.

Livingston, Myra Cohn. 1990. *There Was a Place and Other Poems*. New York: MacMillan.

London, Jonathan. 1998. *Dream Weaver*. Illustrated by Rocco Baviera. San Diego: Harcourt Brace.

Murray, Donald M. 2000. *Writing to Deadline: The Journalist at Work*. Portsmouth, NH: Heinemann.

Nasdijj. 2000. *The Blood Flows Like a River Through My Dreams*. New York: Houghton Mifflin.

Ray, Mary Lynn. 1996. *Mud*. Illustrated by Lauren Stringer. New York: Harcourt Brace.

Ringgold, Faith. 1991. *Tar Beach*. New York: Crown.

Ross, Tony. 1999. *Super Dooper Jezebel*. New York: Econo-Clad Books.

Routman, Regie. 1994. *Invitations*. Portsmouth, NH: Heinemann.

Rylant, Cynthia. 1996. *An Angel for Solomon Singer*. Illustrated by Peter Catalanotto. New York: Orchard Books.

———. 2000. *In November*. Illustrated by Jill Kastner. San Diego: Harcourt Brace.

———. 1998. *The Scarecrow*. Illustrated by Lauren Stringer. San Diego: Harcourt Brace.

Scieszka, Jon. 1989. *The True Story of the Three Little Pigs*. Illustrated by Lane Smith. New York: Puffin.

Shannon, David. 1998. *No, David!* New York: Scholastic.

Steptoe, John. 1986. *Stevie*. New York: HarperTrophy.

Stevenson, James. 1995. *I Had a Lot of Wishes*. New York: Greenwillow.

Tarpley, Natasha. 1998. *I Love My Hair*. Illustrated by E. B. Lewis. New York: Little, Brown.

Viorst, Judith. 1985. *The Pain and the Great One*. Illustrated by Irene Trivas. New York: Dell.

Yashima, Taro. 1955. *Crow Boy*. New York: Viking.

Yolen, Jane. 1987. *Owl Moon*. Illustrated by J. Schoenherr. New York: Philomel.

# Index

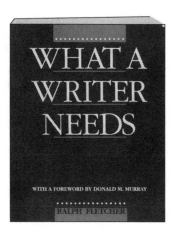